# The Woman's Holistic Guide To Divorce

# The Woman's Holistic Guide To Divorce

### Practical Tips
### for Navigating Legal, Financial,
### and Emotional Decisions

## Wendi Schuller

SUNSTONE PRESS

SANTA FE

The information provided in this book is not intended to substitute for professional medical, psychological, legal, financial, spiritual or other professional advice. You should check with your healthcare provider before taking any nutritional, herbal or homeopathic supplements. Consult with your legal, financial, and health advisers to see what is best in your individual situation.

© 2013 by Wendi Schuller
All Rights Reserved.

All rights reserved. Without limiting the rights under copyrights reserved above, no part of this publication may be reproduced, stored in or introduced into a retrieval system, or transmitted, in any form or by any means (electronic, mechanical, photocopying, recording or otherwise), without the prior written permission of the copyright owner.

Sunstone books may be purchased for educational, business, or sales promotional use. For information please write: Special Markets Department, Sunstone Press, P.O. Box 2321, Santa Fe, New Mexico 87504-2321.

Book and Cover design › Vicki Ahl
Body typeface › Palatino Linotype
Printed on acid-free paper

_____

Library of Congress Cataloging-in-Publication Data

Schuller, Wendi, 1957-
     The woman's holistic guide to divorce : practical tips for navigating legal, financial, and
        emotional decisions / by Wendi Schuller.
        pages cm
     ISBN 978-0-86534-916-2 (softcover : alk. paper)
     1. Divorce. 2. Divorced women. I. Title.
     HQ814.S37 2013
     306.89'3--dc23
                                2013000801

_____

WWW.SUNSTONEPRESS.COM
SUNSTONE PRESS / POST OFFICE BOX 2321 / SANTA FE, NM 87504-2321 /USA
(505) 988-4418 / ORDERS ONLY (800) 243-5644 / FAX (505) 988-1025

# Contents

Thank you to all of the women who shared their stories and wisdom so that many others could have an easier passage through this turbulent time. My gratitude to the attorneys who also provided learned advice which will enable women to avoid many potential pitfalls.

# Introduction

When I was going through my divorce, there were no books on the market providing comprehensive advice on all of the various issues that arose. I was able find some legal advice and also books about children experiencing their own issues revolving around divorce. Financial reports dealing with general tips or investments were available, but they did not give me the nitty gritty information on obtaining interim operating capital/cash. Self-help and improvement advice was in yet another section of the library or bookstore, but they were not specific to divorce.

What is different about *The Woman's Holistic Guide to Divorce* is that in addition to providing comprehensive suggestions for supplements, health remedies and stress reducing support tips, I have also included household hints that can save you a bundle on your newly reduced budget. During the interim period and afterward, some of my girlfriends confided about how they dealt with their families, friends, and in-laws, plus how they were able to let go of this major life event and start anew. There are pointers on how to support your children, both emotionally and financially through this difficult period. These invaluable life tips are a blueprint for change, pertinent to any woman going through a transition, including widows and those facing an empty nest. You will learn about affirmations and coping mechanisms. This is a road map that will help you get through your divorce without feeling alone or uninformed.

You will learn how to select the type of divorce, plus the particular attorney that is best for your situation. Included are many practical tools, such as how to find and save money and how to navigate the minefields of property division. So many of us made mistakes that you can avoid. This book is packed full of stories and juicy tidbits that can be fun, but which are also thought-provoking.

My friends and I developed miscellaneous health issues during and post-divorce. Specific remedies were never addressed in divorce books, nor were choices of supplements to take to alleviate stress. My background as a nurse, Neuro-Linguistic Programming (NLP) practitioner (NLP), plus clinical hypnotherapist brings a more diverse approach to advice. I have talked to many attorneys, plus many divorced people in order to provide practical tips and avoid pitfalls. I pass along spiritual wisdom that helped me to nourish my soul and move forward through this traumatic situation. Advice that you might require is drawn from a plethora of sources in this one book. It may be helpful to skim through the whole book once to get a feel for the types of information that have been provided. After this, then read the book to have your specific needs and questions answered.

The process of divorce is a life-changing event, not just for the individual, but for the whole family, as you leave the familiarity of your previous life and step into an abyss of the unknown. This book provides the safety net and guidance to get you from feeling like a victim to having the skills to gain inner peace and wisdom. As you leave behind uncertainties, inching along the divorce continuum, you learn new strategies to effectively and confidently deal with the legalities and intricacies of divorce.

# 1

## Advice That You Wish Your Girlfriends Could Provide.

Consider marital counseling if there is any chance of salvaging your marriage. Even if that does not solve the problems, then at least you know that you did everything that you could to save your marriage. If your husband will not join you, then go alone. Marital counseling will provide support in this situation and guidance in taking the first few steps. My mother found it invaluable to have a professional confirm what she suspected, that it was time to bail, and she was given concrete measures to achieve this undertaking.

If you have the luxury of time while you are contemplating divorce, then get your financial records and assets in order. One basic action is to make sure that your name is on the deed to your house. In community property states, you still may be able to get your share of the house, even if it is solely in your husband's name.

Here is a sad, but true story. Bella had lived in their house with her husband and their two children for a long time. When she and her husband were divorcing, Bella received a shock. It turned out that her husband's parents legally owned their house, and the parents' names were on the deed. What Bella thought were mortgage payments over the years were essentially deemed rent. They had no other major assets to split in the divorce. Since her husband received income from a family trust fund and had lost his job, that further complicated the alimony and child support issues. Check deeds to make sure that you are an owner and not considered a renter. Be positive that other joint assets, such as cars, stock and investments, have your name on them as well.

Even if a woman does not think she is in a rocky marriage, she should put inheritance or family money gifts into a separate, not a joint account. Do not mix these with other joint accounts or assets. If you do mix them together, you could lose them. In a divorce situation, when kept in a separate account, inheritance and your family's money gifts are considered personal property, not joint assets. Keep in mind that joint accounts, such as checking, can be frozen when one spouse passes on, even when in the middle of a divorce.

A hospital priest insisted that a wife go to the bank when her physician husband had a stroke in the hospital. It was apparent that the physician would not survive, so the priest and another doctor's wife helped this traumatized woman withdraw a large sum of cash from their joint checking account. The priest explained that she would need money to buy food and other necessities for herself and her youngsters. Sure enough, all of their joint accounts were frozen, but this woman did okay, due to a knowledgeable priest.

If many of your financial statements are kept at his or your mutually-owned business, it may be challenging to collect them at a later date, once divorce commences. Right after my ex left me, before the staff was notified, I swooped into our jointly owned business and quickly grabbed what records and personal effects that I could, but only when I knew that my husband would be not be there.

If your husband even only occasionally beats your children, document any marks, such as bruises. Although it was only a few times a year, one father would grab his son so hard that a bruise would form on the boy's arm in the shape of his fingers. The interim psychologist during the divorce turned that father over to the Children, Youth and Family Department (CY&FD). He hired a high-priced attorney who was able to get the investigation closed quickly. CY&FD told the mother that if she had had a picture or two of those bruises, the outcome would have been different.

## Selecting a Divorce Attorney

The next step is finding a divorce attorney. Decide, before hiring a divorce attorney, if you want a courtroom divorce or a collaborative one in the lawyers' offices. Some attorneys do not do both types of divorce. There will be more in a later section of this book about the pros and cons of each type of divorce. The divorce shown in the Disney movie "Enchanted" was the collaborative type.

A tip for finding the right divorce attorney is to approach people that you know or do business with and ask them whom they would recommend for a divorce attorney. A clerk at one retail establishment was adamant that only one lawyer was best. I routinely did business with him and trusted his opinion. That attorney's name started coming up on other people's lists also. I hired her and was quite pleased with my choice. This word-of-mouth inquiry works for finding lawyers in other specialties as well. Check the Better Business Bureau and State Bar Association to see if your selected attorney has any complaints against her. Go online and look up her profile and law firm.

Denny picked an attorney who is one of the nicest, most mild- mannered guys you could ever meet. He is someone you would like as a friend or neighbor. Unfortunately for Denny, this fellow was way too laid back in the court battle with his wife's shark-like attorney. The wife got quite a lot in the divorce, including a big chunk of Denny's business. Instead of a marriage partner, Denny now had an overbearing business partner. When selecting an attorney, make sure to verify the attorney's demeanor in the courtroom.

## Divorce Attorney's Pitfalls

Sometimes one or more names of lawyers who have gouged clients are mentioned. One divorced man, Edward, said to see if anyone mentions sleazy lawyers, so that you know whom to avoid. Just as a great attorney's name may keep popping up, so can a less ethical one, too. During Edward's divorce, he and his wife agreed to a personal property settlement. One of her girlfriends kept telling his wife "you can do much better." Well, Edward's wife got her attorney to ignore the settlement agreement and go after more goods. The judge upheld the original agreement, and the only thing more the wife received was a much larger bill from her attorney. Her lawyer had the reputation of doing what he could to inflate his clients' fees.

In another case, a woman told her attorney just to settle the divorce, because she just wanted to be done with it. Yet it dragged on and on. She contacted her husband, and to her surprise, he had told his attorney the same thing. Her attorney was a money fiend who kept "stirring the pot" to get higher fees. Together, the spouses got the divorce finished more quickly by having a united front when working with their attorneys, who completed the details.

One big divorce tip from my acquaintance, Lenny, is that guys are "programmed to just want to get the divorce over quickly, unless there is anger or revenge involved."

My friend, Sandy, shares this disturbing tidbit about her divorce. The legal fee for Sandy's divorce exactly equaled the amount she received for her share of their house. Interesting.

If you are not pleased with how the attorney's bill is structured, then speak up. Rather than having a total amount for a day or week, have it broken down by tasks or time periods. Instead of having $537.42 for one day, it should be itemized into $97.08 for answering phone calls and $57.30 for emails. Or the bill should state 2:00 pm to 2:30 pm answered and sent emails, $125. In this manner, you will know that your bill isn't being padded.

Maybe there are expenses that you can control better, such as ceasing to send unimportant emails. Could you do some footwork, such as going through bank or investment statements and not paying your attorney's paralegal to do this task?

## Trust Your Gut Instinct

Trust your gut instinct when it tells you something different from your intellect. You may encounter a seemingly ethical person in business or the healing arts, but something just does not seem right. That person appears to be a caring soul, but you seem to feel a little on edge and do not know why. That is your gut instinct letting you know that there is something questionable going on, perhaps at a subconscious level. This is a life tip, not just for divorce situations.

A pleasant lawyer couple that I did business with before my divorce just did not seem right. I would meet one or both of them for coffee or lunch. I felt sorry for the woman, because she did not seem to have any girlfriends. Their billing was lumped into days, rather than by hours, so I was probably charged a lot for my misguided sympathy in meeting that attorney for what I thought were social occasions.

This couple also did some estate work for my mother, but did not want us to come to their office, even for a quick signing of papers. They insisted on meeting us at my office. My mother kept asking them if we were being charged for their time commuting, but she was repeatedly given vague replies. I rue that I didn't mandate a breakdown by time, so I could see whether or not we were charged for unnecessary commutes. I also wonder what I would have found had I seen the inside of their office.

Maybe someone you meet reminds you of a difficult person you knew and alarm bells go off in your head. Well, listening to your gut may prevent you from getting into a sticky situation. That person may remind you of someone else that you do not like because she shares some of her similar devious characteristics.

It is important to select an attorney with whom you can work well as a team. Many women feel it is prudent to consult an attorney when even contemplating a divorce, to obtain astute legal advice and invaluable guidance that can help prepare you for whatever problems that might arise during the divorce.

Some girlfriends have consulted up to four of the best divorce attorneys in town, in order to purposely prevent their spouses from being able to hire these esteemed legal minds. While some attorneys offer a free initial consultation, these savvy women opted to pay the fee instead, thus establishing the confidentiality of a client-attorney relationship. This guarantees that their spouses will not be able to have these lawyers represent them, if their husbands should call their offices at a later point. If you have paid the fee to establish this private client-attorney relationship, but opt not to hire that attorney, then what is said to her or the office staff cannot be used against you later in a divorce situation by your husband. Unfortunately, this works the other way, too. In one case, when a husband already had a girlfriend and wanted out of the marriage quickly, he went to the best divorce attorneys in that city to prevent his wife from hiring them. The other advantage to meeting several lawyers is that you can select the one who clicks with you best. Of course, this can be a costly luxury.

The first point of contact, after the secretary, will be the paralegal who will get your contact information and listen to your story. She will check with the firm's attorneys to make sure that there is not a conflict of interest in accepting you as a client. If your chosen attorney, or possibly another partner, had any dealings with your husband, they may not be able to accept your case. The paralegal will ask some questions to clarify your situation. The next step is that she may get the attorney on the phone for a brief encounter or just to schedule a face-to-face meeting.

At your first meeting: bring the following documents and information:

Any bank and financial statements, including tax returns.
Your childrens' social security numbers and financial records.
Your pre-nup agreement, if applicable.
The history of your marriage. Any affairs? Did you hire a detective?

Any alcohol or drug abuse? Any mental illness?
Any physical, or emotional abuse?

Take notes during your first meeting, to review later, when you are less stressed. This information made my initial encounter go smoothly, and enabled my attorney to quickly grasp my situation.

# 2

## Women In Transition

*C*all your United Way to see what community resources are available to you. Other good sources to contact are a women's health center or the local community college. Ask specifically for support groups or classes for women getting a divorce. Some community colleges have a course named "Women in Transition," which is excellent for recent widows, empty nesters and those going through a divorce. The class meets for around three hours a week and the women have a confidentiality agreement (written or oral), where everything said in the class stays there. Women can discuss their most personal feelings, relay traumas and receive understanding from their supportive classmates and instructors. It is a safe environment to express oneself and to gain personal insight.

The "Women in Transition" class features at least one speaker a week on a myriad of subjects, ranging from fitness to finances and qualifying for a mortgage. The CPA discussed ways to elevate our credit rating and erroneous actions which lowered it. The psychologist was excellent and gave concrete strategies for managing stress, including court hearings. She gave practical tips on how to deal with difficult people in our lives. We had some homework between classes, which increased our awareness and problem solving abilities regarding our personal situations.

The support and friendship from the classmates makes going through heartbreaking, stressful situations a lot easier. The group and speakers are like a life preserver is being thrown out to you in turbulent water. These classes run six to eight weeks, and people often want to stay in touch after the class ends. Even if you feel that you have it all together, please consider enrolling in this valuable class.

There are support groups for women that meet regularly to discuss various issues. If there is not one specifically for divorce, it still can be worthwhile to check out this type of assistance. In the movie "Starting Over" with Burt Reynolds, Candace Bergen, and Jill Claiborne, there are humorous scenes with both men's and women's support groups. The movie really shows the difference between genders in an enjoyable way.

Unfortunately, my lawyer did not know of any support in the community for women going through divorce. Others lawyers that I discussed this with were also unaware of the "Women in Transition" course. Do not rely on your attorney to help you in this area.

Many women find that their religious faith is a source of comfort and guidance during turbulent times. Kiki said that she reads the "Book of Psalms" when she has questions or strife, and opens the Bible and points to a random verse. Invariably, it contains the just the answer that she was seeking. Carrie is currently going through a divorce and became more active in her church, doing the Gospel readings during Mass. In lieu of a support group, some women have opted to join a ladies' group at their place of worship. I have met some wonderful ministers' wives who embody the concept of unconditional love and who listen to many confidences. It is important to take the path that feels most comfortable for you.

Another source for help is your local Rape Crisis Center. Ours does free counseling for women and children who have been in abusive situations. They do great work with Post Traumatic Stress Disorder (PTSD), teaching concrete strategies for dealing with the triggers. Women and children from abusive marriages can have PTSD, and it is imperative to receive help to avoid, or learn to minimize, its triggers. The Rape Crisis Center greatly assisted me in decreasing my insomnia and enabled me to minimize stress in post-divorce courtroom hearings. They even sent a support person (advocate) to go with me during an especially difficult court hearing.

# 3

## Types of Divorces

### Collaborative Divorce

Q. What is collaborative divorce and why would I want one?

A. Collaborative divorce meetings are usually in one of the attorney's conference rooms and include the husband and wife, in addition to their attorneys. Instead of having a judge settle disputes, the different outcomes of issues are decided upon by the four people present. No case is pleaded, nor is a judge's decision made. The solutions to the problems are immediate, with no waiting six weeks until the next court date.

There is give and take in this more pleasant atmosphere of lattes and pastries. I was lucky to be able to cuddle my attorney's young kitten during many of the meetings. Her purr had a magic effect on my tense or hostile feelings.

In a collaborative divorce, all information is shared with full disclosure. Life coaches may be recommended by the attorneys, and they are allowed to be present at the meetings for the support of each spouse. You can brainstorm together for creative solutions which may not occur to a judge. Small pet peeves can be dealt with here, especially those that would be too trivial for a courtroom.

Q. What if my husband abused me and I quake in his presence?

A. The spouses can be in separate rooms with the attorneys going between them. In my case, my husband was placed across the table catty-corner from me, and we were never left alone together in the room. If I came early, I hung out in the paralegal's room until everyone else arrived for the meeting. The requirement of collaborative divorce is to agree not to threaten to take the other spouse to court. The goal is to quickly resolve issues, divide assets, and do a custody evaluation without court intervention.

At one point, my husband terminated our collaborative process and we were required to get new attorneys and a financial adviser before duking it out in court. When he discovered the monumental difference in cost, my husband wanted to go back to the collaborative process. Luckily, our two original collaborative attorneys and financial adviser took us back and we proceeded where we had left off previously.

Q. What if I blow my top? Will that end the collaborative process?

A. Your attorney is trained to read body language in case you forget to ask for a break. If you start feeling out of control, there are a few options. Say you have to go to the ladies room and then yell inside the toilet stall. Get an ice cold glass of water to cool you down a bit. You may ask to speak privately with your attorney.

Q. Who are the advisers in a collaborative divorce?

A. Consultants, such as a financial adviser and a child psychologist, are selected jointly by the two attorneys. They are present at only some of the divorce conferences. I found that the neutral financial adviser was the most important person to have around during the divorce proceedings, even more so than my attorney. She quickly got down to the nitty gritty and divided the assets fairly.

Q. What are the pitfalls of collaborative divorce?

A. On rare occasions, a collaborative divorce attorney may withdraw from the process if he discovers that his client has been hiding assets or has performed unethical acts. If this is the case, the divorce process has to start again from the beginning. If one spouse drops out of the collaborative process, then none of the findings or any of the information gained can be used in another divorce proceeding or in court, nor can the original consultants take part in future court hearings. You literally have to start from ground zero and lose the money invested in the earlier collaborative proceedings.

Q. My husband is well known, so would the collaborative process be right for me?

A. Your husband may be a celebrity or known by judges and court personnel. Judges are supposed to be neutral, but they are humans, after all, and can show favoritism. If you live in a small community, it may not be possible to get a judge who has not heard of either of you. In the collaborative process, all decisions are made by the spouses, with their lawyers' guidance. It doesn't matter if one's husband is the mayor, as the wife's attorney will advise and protect her.

## Courtroom Divorce or Litigation

Testifying in court can be traumatic, including being ridiculed by a spouse. Husbands and wives can have that "winner take all" attitude or act as though the courtroom is an arena for a devastating match of wits. Adversarial divorce may close the door on exes working together post-divorce on various issues that might arise.

Some husbands or wives have made it through the court system with no complaints. Patrick's wife was a model who had a wild affair which led him to file for divorce in a southern state. The judge told the adulteress to take her clothes and personal items out of their house. The husband wound up with everything else. Patrick would not have gotten such a rich settlement if he had used the collaborative process and was quite happy with the outcome of his court case. Depending upon where you reside, a court judge may be more sympathetic to a spurned spouse.

## Costs Involved

With both types of divorce, you will be required to pay a retainer to your newly hired attorney, and in my case, I paid $5,000. Collaborative divorce is a lot less costly than a court divorce. There are typically four to seven sessions before the divorce is finalized. It can take over a year to complete a litigation divorce. After I paid the initial retainer, subsequent payments to my attorney were taken from "the community pot," not from me directly. As property and other assets were sold, the consultants and both attorneys got paid, and the leftover money was divided between us. I was out of a job during part of the divorce, since we had a jointly owned and run business. The money that came into the business during our divorce was still a community asset, so some of the lawyer's fees were taken from that. This is particularly good for stay-at-home moms or working women who make significantly less that their husbands.

The first stages of litigation are determining both the actual complaint and what one wants to attain from the divorce, such as alimony. The papers are then served to the other spouse. In Leonard's case, he and his wife were on very good terms and mutually decided upon a divorce. They had discussed their marital situation, realizing that they would get along better as friends than spouses. Leonard was quite shocked and hurt when his wife had divorce papers delivered to him at work, in front of clients and co-workers. He kept saying that all his wife had to do was to call him and he would have come and gotten them. This set the tone for an adversarial divorce. If you are on the receiving end of divorce papers, read them carefully. There may be a hearing date or specified time limit in which to respond.

In the collaborative process, you will present your monthly expenses, and a temporary amount will be paid to you by your husband. This is called interim support. In litigation, the court may freeze assets so that they cannot be sold, cashed in or hidden. As in collaborative, litigation will impose some restrictions, such as not changing the beneficiary of a life insurance policy. You are probably the beneficiary pre-divorce, so this prevents your husband from changing it to his girlfriend once divorce proceedings commence. If he dies mid-divorce, you then are protected.

The following stage in litigation divorce is the discovery, where all assets are put on the table. Financial records and other information are shared between attorneys, so that the property can later be divided. Negotiations may end in a settlement, and if not, the divorce case goes before a judge, who makes the final decision.

An option is to hire your own personal financial advisor to check over this aspect of your divorce. Although there may be one already working with both attorneys, it may bring you peace of mind to have your own adviser to go over details with you between meetings/court dates.

If an agreement is not reached, then you and your lawyer next prepare for court. Whoever initiated the divorce appears first before the judge. The other party follows, presenting his/her side. After the evidence is presented and expert witnesses are heard, then the lawyers present their legal arguments before the judge. The judge then makes a ruling (decision), which is the divorce decree.

# Mediation

Mediation is gaining in popularity as another option to complete a divorce, at a fraction of the normal cost. You have probably read about neighbors going to mediation over a tree that is blocking another one's view, or leaves blowing onto their property. Some condo associations and tenants settle problems through mediation.

The mediator is a neutral person with extensive training in negotiation, who works with both the husband and the wife to divide assets and complete the divorce process. Just as with the other types of divorce, spouses bring financial and tax records, plus any other pertinent information to these meetings.

At the first meeting, you will go over rules, just as in collaborative sessions, such as no threats, yelling or recording the sessions. Goals will be discussed and you will be asked about your relationship and the desired outcome of the divorce.

Mediation does especially well in amicable divorces, where the spouses may want to stay in touch afterwords. In mediation, there is more dialogue, so everyone has a better comprehension of the reasons behind what each spouse wants. This gives the three of you a better understanding of each spouse's positions, so that compromises can be reached. A mediator works with both parties together, typically in three sessions. A fair distribution of assets and resolution of other issues are accomplished within these sessions.

You do not have to go it alone through mediation, but can have an attorney guide you from behind the scenes, although not at the sessions. You attend the mediation sessions with just your spouse. Your lawyer can give you advice and also review any documents from the mediation negotiations. It is possible to just hire an attorney to review the final contract before it is signed. This saves a bundle of money, because you get the benefit of an attorney's advice and strategies without paying for her time in the actual mediation sessions.

Some women have hired their own financial advisors to look over the preliminary financial and alimony settlement before signing anything. You may be advised to tweak retirement benefits or do a more advantageous trade of assets.

## Do it Yourself Divorce

A couple with a non-contested divorce who wants to do it on the cheap can get the required documents plus legal advice online for only $299. The price is 100% refundable if the court does not accept these divorce papers. There is a comprehensive guide and step-by-step process to enable you both to complete this task. There are other online sites offering free divorce forms.

A friend bought a book with legal advice and divorce forms. She offered to take a little less of their joint assets, just to get her husband to agree to file for divorce in this way. She nabbed a judge in the hallway and the whole process cost her $75. Her husband had family wealth and she did not want an expensive court battle with his high-priced lawyers. She may have gotten alimony if she had had a more traditional divorce, but was willing to give that up just to get out of the marriage quickly and cheaply.

# 4

## Common Questions in Divorce

Girlfriends have dealt with a plethora of various issues during their divorce. Here is a medley of questions and solutions.

Q. When can I change the locks?

A. You can change the locks during the divorce, but talk to your lawyer first. If your husband has moved out, but the kids and you hear someone roaming around the house at 2 am, turn on a lot of lights and make noise. You want to make sure it is not a burglar. If that is a possibility, then call 911. After the second night in a row that we heard a person moving around in our house in the wee hours of the morning, I called my attorney. She gave me permission, so the locksmith and alarm companies came out that evening. The locks and codes were changed, including my garage door opener. I did this during the first week after hiring my divorce attorney. In abuse or fear situations, it is essential for your family's safety and well-being to change those locks as soon possible. Of course, if you are getting a restraining order or if there has been abuse, your lawyer may say to have this done right away. Your lawyer would inform your husband of the locks being changed, and then make arrangements for him to retrieve his belongings.

If you are in amicable divorce proceedings, you still may want to have the locks changed, because your husband may have given spare sets of keys to people that you do not want coming into your house.

If your soon-to-be ex wants something that he left behind, there are several options:

You can leave it outside at a predetermined time.

Your attorney's paralegal can meet your husband with your new set of keys, let him in to the house and watch what he removes.

If you are friendly, you can invite him in for a cup of coffee while he gathers up his things.

Q. I am just not up to having house guests during my divorce. How do I handle this and not cause hard feelings?

A. It is hard to say "No" to a relative or friend, if they have been staying at your house regularly. Tell them about changes or new rules and let THEM decide not to visit. For example, an elderly relative, without kids, stayed with me every Christmas, and sometimes in the summer. She wanted to be wined, dined and entertained and, like a fool, I did it. Even right before Christmas, I would be taking her to holiday parties and concerts. She wanted to go to the December 26th sales, so I would leave my young tots to hit the shops with her. Right after 9/11 happened, I told this relative that my friends and I had a wakeup call to do more things with our kids. (I made it less personal by including friends.) I informed her that on Christmas, the whole focus would be on the children and what they wanted to do. She was told that we would watch Christmas shows on TV, read stories, or just hang out while the boys enjoyed their Christmas season. I did not tell her that she could not come, but she found somewhere else that she needed to be at that time that year, and ever since.

Some people who live near the beach tell acquaintances that it is great that they will be in town and to please save a night or two for a get-together. That is friendly, yet makes it clear that they are not running a hotel. Others give a time limit up front, such as three days, due to work or court hearings. You can say, "Are you renting a car, or do you want me to get a bus schedule, so that you can go places while I am at work?" Some people honestly forget that hosts still have to go to work or don't want to use up valuable vacation time when guests are present.

Q. I usually host the holiday family dinners and just do not feel like it now, especially during my divorce. How do I get out of it?

A. If you do not feel up to hosting a family get-together, suggest meeting at a reasonably priced restaurant. If this is not acceptable, then be honest and let your family know that with your divorce, you just cannot do it. Ask how a holiday family get-together could be made easier. Perhaps a cousin would do the event if it were a brunch instead of a dinner. This is the time to bring up rotating family holiday events and have it be a pot luck, with the host mainly supplying the home, dishes and utensils.

Another option is to go away for the holidays. Holiday cruises are fun, festive and no one has to cook or clean. Other family members may want to join you, and perhaps you could all get a special group rate.

Q. I cannot seem to communicate with my teenager now. Any hints?

Be direct and to the point when communicating with teenagers. When dining in a restaurant, say "Elbows," instead of "I am sick and tired of your manners. Even a first grader knows not to put his elbows on a table in a restaurant." Use one word or a short phrase to convey your message. Teens tune us out quickly.

Leave a short note, written in a lively color of marker, taped to the bathroom mirror. For example, "Please change the litter box" written in neon orange will grab his attention.

When they are required to do a task, give a time frame. If the response is, "Yeah, I'll do it later," then get a firm time commitment. Ask what time the task will commence, so you will not nag. If he says "nine o'clock," then do not give time reminders, such as "It is fifteen minutes until nine." After the first several times, the teen gets the job done by a certain time, knowing you will not be on his case about it.

Ask your teen to take a walk with you, or do something athletic. Often this will be the time where he opens up about what is on his mind.

# 5

## Breaking the News

### Telling your children about your imminent divorce

You may want to break the news of your divorce to your children with your spouse present, reassuring them that they are loved. By both of you. Explain that details have yet to be worked out, but they will be able to spend time with each parent. Do not pass blame onto the other parent, even if a third party is involved. State the facts as calmly as possible.

My husband left a "Dear John" note that the children and I both read. I could not reach him by phone, but I did catch his mother, who confirmed the contents of the note. Ideally, you and your children do not find out about your husband's departure at the same time.

You may want to tell your parents privately, plus also have a chat with your in-laws. When spreading this news, set the tone on how you want others to respond. Surprisingly, I vacillated between shock and euphoria, so I presented the news in a positive frame. Friends acknowledged my shock and gave me nurturing, positive support.

Some women are a mixed bag of feelings and require sorting these out first, before sharing anything with the rest of the world. I am a wee bit Irish and have heard of other Irish women taking to their beds for a few days when bad news strikes. I was blindsided by my husband's departure, but discovered quickly how much I hoped it was permanent. I hired my divorce attorney exactly a week later. Whatever you are feeling is okay.

### In-laws

During your divorce, consider pulling back from your in-laws to create space. If you love your husband's family and want to continue your relationship post-divorce, keep your divorce details private. They may feel conflicted because "blood is thicker than water." They also could reveal confidences which may add to the divorce conflict. The in-laws may feel that their son is being unfairly persecuted, so keep mum.

If your in-laws are not abusive, reassure them that you want them to continue to be an important part of your children's lives. Grandparents can be invaluable with providing a loving, neutral space for children. It is in everyone's best interest when grandparents can give nonjudgmental support to kids during this difficult time.

Unfortunately, some grandparents may choose to sever all contact with their grandkids. In one case, the grandfather was very passive, but during visitation, his wife would loudly proclaim the perceived faults of the boys' mother. Due to paternal abuse, the older son stopped visitation and the younger one had court-mandated supervised ones. Eventually, the younger son was allowed to stop his visitation. The grandparents told the boys that they would only have contact if they resumed a relationship with their father. Luckily, the boys had a wonderful, loving grandmother, plus other elderly family friends who filled the vacant positions.

## Mutual Friends

A tricky situation is how to deal with mutual friends. Your spouse's co-workers and college buddies will align with him. Be careful with couples where you are friends with the wife and your spouse with her husband. Your friend may inadvertently pass along juicy tidbits about your situation to her husband, who then tells your spouse. This could gum up the works in a contentious divorce.

I did call some of the spouses of my husband's colleagues at the beginning of our divorce. I thought it was best that these women heard the news from me directly, particularly since he wrote that "Dear John" letter. This interaction made it much easier to chat with these ladies post-divorce, although we did not formally socialize again.

Be cautious with whom you share your divorce details. People do talk and may not realize that their co-worker or neighbor knows your spouse. This could come back to "bite you in the butt," as my attorney warned.

At a women's luncheon, I discussed my pending divorce with two women whom I know did not pass along anything. However, someone eavesdropped and called my husband, who was furious, and brought this up at the next divorce session. I permanently dropped out of that organization and learned not to discuss private issues in a public setting.

## 6

# Children During Divorce

A girlfriend's tip: If the sudden announcement of one's husband wanting a divorce leaves a woman incapacitated, have a loving, neutral person, like a godmother, take the kids for a day or more. They will have positive support, an ear to confide in, plus maybe some fun diversions.

Reinforce to your children that they are not in any way to blame for the divorce. Do not put down the other parent. Perhaps just avoid talking about him in general. Children know that their other parent has faults and they do not require them to be cataloged. Under no circumstances say, "You are just like your father." It serves no purpose, even if you mean it as a compliment.

I knew that my father had mental health issues and my mother periodically stated, "You are just like your father." I thought that I also was mentally ill up until I went away to college. Then I discovered how healthy, strong and sane I really was.

Remember that you are a parent and not a good buddy. Continue to enforce boundaries and rules. Jacqueline Kennedy stated, "If you bungle raising your children, I don't think whatever else you do well matters very much."

In parenting classes (that you may be required to attend), one learns not to have the children pass messages to the other parent during visitation. Kids feel put on the spot, especially if these youngsters know they are the bearer of bad news. Take what the child says about the other parent "with a grain of salt." When I was around five, I would tell my father that my mother had a maid. It was purely wishful thinking.

Do not ask how visitation went or what your son and and the other parent did. Your child may not want to admit that he had a fun day at the amusement park in order to spare your feelings, especially if it looks like you have been crying.

Reassure children that you will receive interim support during the divorce. Give the kids some control in this unsettling situation. Ask, "How can we cut our spending?" When children are involved in solutions, they are happier complying with new financial strategies. You would be surprised at how creative little ones can be. Look on the ground for money. We seem to find enough for ice cream treats. Eat out for breakfast instead of dinner. Use public transportation.

Other girlfriends' tips: have a pizza and family night at home. Rent or borrow a DVD from the library and heat up a frozen pizza. Papa Murphy's has fresh, made-to-order pizzas that you pick up and bake later. Take a picnic lunch by a river or to a lovely park.

Other people have called the Chamber of Commerce, or have gone online to discover what free events and festivals are happening in their communities. It is important to establish a new bond with your children, one that does not include the presence of your husband.

Have potluck suppers with other single moms and kids. I often meet my friends at coffee shops, split a pastry and catch up with gossip. It is a lot cheaper than a full meal.

If your family asks what to get you and the kids for Christmas, suggest that they pool their gifts into one and buy a gift card to Disneyland. At my local grocery store, there are three day hopper passes to Disney for around $165. That would be a fabulous way to forget about the divorce for a few days.

## Adult Offspring

Even adult offspring may feel as much adrift as younger ones. They may be married and have their own children, yet feel caught in your tug of war. Do not expect them to be your confidantes; call your girlfriends instead. Do not ask them to be witnesses in litigation, as my stepmother did to me. (I turned down this request.) Counseling can be a beneficial tool for children of all ages.

Adult offspring may feel grief at losing their childhood home and the other changes taking place. They may need space from both parents to work through these swirling emotions. Talk with them about what they are experiencing, how they are feeling about it, and what they need to help them feel better.

## Pets

Remember that your pets feel emotions and can pick up on the anxieties and anger in their environment. Cats and dogs may be facing a change in residence as part of your divorce. They do not understand what is happening, so they may require more TLC and attention. Taking your dog on extra walks will increase your exercise, thus improving your health and well-being. Various studies have indicated that one can lower their blood pressure and calm their nervous system when petting cats. Their purr induces relaxation. Maybe enlist the kids to provide some additional playtime for Rover and Tigger.

## Stepmothers in Divorce

When my stepmother divorced my father, I was in college, so it was very easy to maintain contact with her and the extended family. Since I could drive, I popped in and continued to enjoy family activities. My step-grandparents, aunts, uncles and cousins treated me in the same loving way post-divorce.

Avoid making ultimatums to your children. When I was 21, my father was quite annoyed that I stayed in contact with his former wife and family. He gave me the ultimatum that it was either him or them. I chose them.

When my father died, I was not able to attend the funeral home viewing, but I did attend the funeral. My mother and stepmother went to the viewing together. My mother gleefully proclaimed to his former co-workers and friends that they were "members of the former wives club."

If you have young stepchildren and are divorcing, be sure to address visitations as part of your divorce decree. There are creative solutions. If your husband is going to have them every other week, then maybe you could see them for one of those visits, such as part of a Saturday. If you have an amicable relationship with their biological mother, then offer to see the children and give their mom a break.

One woman's magazine had a story about how these two girls loved their stepmother. After their own mother died, these young girls insisted that their dad and stepmom move into their house. When the dad and stepmother got a divorce, the girls lived with their stepmother in their mother's house. The happy ending was a photograph of the now young ladies escorting their beloved stepmother down the aisle at her wedding.

## Visitation

Unless you have an amicable divorce situation, have a neutral drop off and return place. I chose an assigned drop-off place, as it was too stressful for my sons and me to have their father drop them off at my house. I did not want him around my property. The boys tended to fly out of his car before it even stopped. Some fathers have been late with pick-ups and drop-offs, and the kids have had to wait by a window, watching for his car. This can impact your plans, especially if you are meeting people for a show. If this happens, ask him to call you beforehand, if he is running late, so you have the option of making a new arrangement.

If the drop-off place for older children is a public place, such as a coffee shop, then their father is more likely to pick them up on time to avoid public embarrassment. After the second time he is late for a pick- up, or if the kids are returned late, contact your attorney to have visitation enforced or modified. During and also post-divorce, treat any interaction with their father as if it were a business situation. State facts and keep your emotions out of it.

The first several times of visitation will be especially difficult, so decide if you would rather be alone or be distracted by your pals. During the second visitation, I was in a small shop and just lost it. The sales clerk, bless her heart, acted like nothing was different and finished our transaction. I finally blurted out about visitation. She had already guessed that was the problem and proceeded to tell me of her experiences with her young tots. This young woman assured me that future visitations would get easier, and she was right.

Emma has these words of wisdom: "Alone is different from being lonely." The difference between the two is that she felt victimized when she was feeling lonely. Realization brought the concept that quiet time (being alone) is nice. During visitation, when her two sons were with their father, Emma learned that she could use that time for spiritual growth and meditation. Emma felt "poor me" at first, but has a different perspective now. Your "story" (past) takes root in childhood and influences the way you see the world and your particular situation. She felt that her divorce experience was much worse than it had to be due to not letting go of her "story." Emma had been adopted and her divorce triggered abandonment issues.

# 7

## Surviving the Holidays

Here are some tips on surviving Christmas and other holidays without your kids while in a divorce situation. Even if you do not have any children, your holidays will be quite different during and post-divorce. I got some wonderful British magazines, such as *Woman and Home*, *Good Housekeeping UK* and *Red* as a present to myself. After we had a lovely Christmas morning at home, my two sons left with their father. I had uninterrupted time, which I spent drinking tea and reading these cheery magazines. I sat near the Christmas tree with my cats, and the afternoon without my kids flew by comfortably.

My mother's tip is to work on Christmas. She worked in a hospital and then a nursing home, both being festive places with yummy food and parties. My mother liked my stepmother, so she knew that I was having fun with her family on holidays when I was there during visitation.

Do you have any single friends who get together on holidays? After being married for so long, you may not know what they do at Christmas time or Thanksgiving. What do your other divorced friends do on holidays? Maybe you could all rent a chick flick and have a little spiked nog to increase your holiday spirit. If your family lives nearby, spend time with them.

Some women get a lot of satisfaction helping out at a homeless shelter on Thanksgiving and Christmas. Animals at shelters or rescue groups still need to eat or have litter boxes changed. My older son seems to have to do this duty on holidays for his cat rescue group.

There are a plethora of charities that especially need help over the holidays. In the UK, Contact the Elderly, has monthly get-togethers for elderly people living alone. Their Christmas parties are extra festive, with carols, presents, yummy food and sherry. Some volunteers have formed closed bonds with the aged person assigned to them, and also claim to get a tremendous personal benefit from helping out with this charity. You may want to see what volunteer options are available in your area.

Start new family traditions, after getting input from your children on what they especially would like to do. Mix the old traditions with new ones. We have a nice brunch at home on Thanksgiving Day, while watching the

Macy's parade. Then it is off to a movie, followed by a simple pot roast dinner at home later. We used to go to an over-priced restaurant on Thanksgiving, but now enjoy our new tradition much better.

Be glad that you do not have to go to all those time-consuming holiday cocktail parties now, as you did when still married. Just think of the fun things you can do with the kids post-divorce with that extra time. Make a gingerbread house from a kit, bake festive cookies for gifts, eat pizza in PJs and watch "Elf" or "White Christmas."

One divorced friend got me spa products for Christmas so I could pamper myself in peace when my boys went to their father's house. Another newly divorced mother got a best-seller and waited until the kids went to their father's, to dive into the book.

If you have shared custody, when your children will be away for a week or two, go out of town. Friends who have been to the European Christmas markets rave about these trips. Go on a Viking River Cruise in Germany and you will be around many other people during this festive time.

When you are alone on a ship, you are far more likely to reach out to other people and make new friends. As a new divorcee, Kim went on a Cunard Line ship for a Christmas cruise and enjoyed the festivities, holiday shows, food, plus being with the other passengers. It was fun for her to attend a big, black tie bash for New Year's Eve and not need a date.

I have heard about a few women who have told friends and family that they were going away for the holidays, but really holed up at home, enjoying the solitude.

# 8

## Expert Advisers in a Divorce

### Child Psychologist

The lawyers may want a child psychologist on board to set up interim visitation. She may initially meet both the parents and the children to get a sense of the family dynamics. In a contentious divorce, the parents have individual consultations, where the children are met separately. The psychologist does not do therapy, but may give suggestions or strategies to enable the children to have a smoother transition between parental homes and to teach them how to deal with visitation. She monitors visitation to make sure that the situation is suitable. At the beginning, behavior expectations are announced, such as the parents not putting each other down and limiting divorce discussions in front of the kids. If there are any violations or issues, these are addressed.

In one case, a woman had told her in-laws before divorce that she felt a particular movie and play were too raunchy for children. Soon after her divorce started, her mother-in-law got tickets to take her sons to see the play during a visitation. The younger son, particularly, was quite upset by the play, so the child psychologist was called in after the visitation.

The interim child psychologist may recommend to the attorneys and parents that the children start therapy with another psychologist. Also, if abuse is discovered, then the child psychologist is bound by law to turn over the offending parent to a child protection agency, so they can make an official determination.

Before or at the beginning of your divorce, ask around to see if there is a particularly good or less effective child psychologist. I found out the hard way that four other mothers would have loved to tar and feather the interim child psychologist that our attorneys had jointly selected. She was the sweetest person, someone you would select as a new best friend. However, this psychologist saw the world through "rose colored glasses," a bit out of touch with reality. She looked and acted the part Amy Adams played in Disney's "Enchanted" movie. This professional wanted overnight visitations when the boys could not handle short daytime ones. If she had determined custody, it would have been a disaster.

Most likely, the court or the interim psychologist will mandate that both parents attend a parenting class and may specify a certain one. The parents attend them at different times to avoid conflict. I got more out of listening to the other parents and how the instructors helped them deal with individual situations than I did with the actual content taught. It was so helpful to hear the fathers' perspectives regarding visitation, divorce proceedings and other issues. I gained a wider understanding about many things. The camaraderie was great, and this was a safe place to vent and gain self-awareness.

## Children's Therapist

Both parents have to agree upon a psychologist to do the therapy for the children. Again, do a word of mouth survey, or ask your pediatrician whom she recommends. I highly urge you to find a psychologist who is strong, and who would be willing to go to court, if necessary, for your child's best interest. My sons' therapist has gone to court several times post-divorce, as an advocate for my younger son regarding visitation. A mother, who also had a bad time with the same interim psychologist, had suggested this therapist, who stepped in during her divorce and changed the visitation schedule for her son. I was very glad that I followed her advice.

## Custody Evaluator

It may be that you and your spouse agree upon visitation times with your attorney's support. The interim visitation schedule set up by the psychologist may work all right and custody can be based from this. However, if it is unsatisfactory, then the attorneys may get a formal custody evaluation performed by a qualified psychologist (one who does this regularly for the court). This is a good way to proceed, if you feel that custody and visitation arrangements are not going well. Talk to your attorney about bringing this professional on board. We had to pay the custody evaluator $8,000 up front, and the whole process took several weeks, with a binding parenting plan issued.

The custody evaluator meets with the parents together for the first time, or separately, in abusive situations. She will spend time interviewing each parent to obtain a marital and parenting history. I gave a copy of the one I did for the initial meeting with my attorney. Then parents and children will do a battery of personality tests, including the MMPI (Minnesota Multiphasic Personality Inventory) and the Rorschach inkblots test, where the child creates a story to go with a picture.

Parents will have a chance to refute any allegations made by the other spouse and state their wishes for custody. You and your attorney will meet with the custody evaluator, and so will your husband and his attorney at another time. The recommendations will be presented in the parenting plan.

## Life Coach

Your attorneys, or the interim psychologist, may recommend that one or both of you see a life coach to talk over your concerns and make sure you are on the right path. A life coach does not do therapy, but rather helps you problem-solve if you feel stuck. She can help you form concrete strategies, such as how to go about looking for a job. She may have you draw a circle (pie chart) and divide it into different aspects of your life, such as time spent doing various endeavors. This helps you gain perspective on priorities if one segment of your life is greatly diminished. A life coach may be allowed to come to divorce hearings in order to give you support.

## Financial Adviser

The attorneys will obtain a financial adviser, who is especially qualified to work in divorce cases, to go over your joint assets. She will be invaluable in digging through financial records and fairly dividing these assets. Everything is laid out on the table, including the blue book worth of your vehicles. Loans are tricky and may be put on one person's side, if he will be getting significant property later, once the loan is paid. Or all loans may be paid off, including credit cards and mortgages, and the difference given to the spouses at the conclusion of the divorce. It is in your best interest to fully cooperate with this adviser.

This financial adviser will probably attend all of your divorce sessions, unless one is specifically for visitation. She will draw up lists of assets and assist with the determination of interim support. There is a formula for alimony and child support based on income, so she may help less in this area. She may be the one paying joint bills from the community pot, such as to workers renovating a jointly owned house being prepared for sale during the divorce. Money from assets sold during the divorce is put in a trust fund, and checks are issued for joint expenses from this account. Bills are paid to lawyers and advisers, and for work being done to get assets sold.

If she finds that some assets appear missing or if there are questions, then a forensic accountant or even an investigator may be hired. Sometimes a forensic investigator is used in determining personal and business assets to make sure everything is on the up and up. Your husband may have transferred money from your joint account to a friend or relative. If he does jobs where he gets paid in cash, look into the existence of a safety deposit box.

# 9

## Parenting Plan

A custody evaluator will write a parenting plan which is entered in court as part of the divorce decree. It spells out visitation amounts and sharing or alternating holidays, and type of custody. One parent can have physical custody, which means that the children live with one parent but may have some visitation with the other parent. I was given physical custody, where my sons lived with me, but they also had some daytime only visitation with their father. Joint custody means that both parents make decisions regarding their children's school, religion and healthcare. Joint custody can still be awarded, even if one parent is in jail, as he can still be consulted on these issues.

If parents are having a contentious divorce, the parenting plan may appoint a mediator, listed as the "court monitor," to handle all communication between the parents post-divorce. He sends or forwards emails, such as trips planned and any other communication. In many divorces, the other parent has to be informed if the children will be taken across state lines. If, when a child reaches eighteen and does not want to continue visitation, the court monitor deals with this situation, notifying the other parent, and possibly finding a person to supervise the younger one's visitations.

The parenting plan may stipulate the percentage that each parent pays for therapy and medical bills. It may also prevent either parent from calling Children's Protective Services on the other one, but instead, may have complaints go through the court monitor to determine justification. If there is a basis for an allegation, then he would contact the appropriate agency. In acrimonious divorce, specifics, such as neither parent talking about the other parent, can be addressed.

Whether it is stipulated in the parenting plan or in the divorce decree, address college expenses. Make sure that your spouse will pay for all, or least a certain percentage of tuition, room and board and other fees. Have it stipulated that this includes grad school as well. If your husband balks at having to pay college expenses, be creative. See if he would do a lump sum after high school graduation, paid directly to the university. This could be a tax write-off. Or maybe he would be willing to open a 529 plan for each child, which is a savings account that is solely for a child's educational expenses.

An unfortunate new trend is to mandate reconciliation therapy with an abusive or estranged parent, after the parent has undergone counseling. This process is formally set up with each person having a different therapist to work together to achieve this endeavor. Strongly oppose this, because if the children want to have a reconciliation with the abusive parent, this is possible without being mandated by the court. In one case, more abuse was revealed by both children after the divorce. Yet, one nutty judge tried to enforce the parenting plan, by mandating that the reconciliation therapy still take place. The younger child was still in visitation, so it was costly for his mother and time intensive for the child's therapist to thwart this court ruling.

## 10

## Pitfalls of Self-medication

Do not fall into the trap of self-medicating to alleviate the emotional pain of divorce. It does not eliminate the past; it just postpones it in a destructive way. It does not allow you to clearly and deeply process and release these emotions. Taking illicit drugs, alcohol or too much prescription medication is detrimental to your body, spirit and to those around you.

Cathy was happily married, with a young daughter, and building a dream house with her husband. They regularly entertained, rode horses, did community service and had a great life. Cathy had overcome a drinking problem in the past and was a fragile person who felt life's blows acutely. Her husband took some business trips out of state and met a married woman in his line of work. This woman previously had an affair, then divorced her husband to marry her lover. Cathy received a phone call from the other woman's husband when their spouses were having an affair. Cathy could not cope and began a downward spiral with alcohol. Cathy's husband divorced her and married the other woman, who moved into the dream house. The couple deviously campaigned to obtain full custody of the daughter and were successful, partly due to Cathy's increased drinking. Cathy's parents helped tremendously, but she still had a breakdown and was put on medication. This drama continued, culminating when the new wife refused to let the daughter call her mother on Mother's Day. By now the daughter was older and possibly could have called her mother surreptitiously. A few days later, Cathy took an unintentional overdose of prescription medication, compounded by alcohol, and died.

Enjoying a margarita with the girls, or having a glass of wine while watching a chick flick, is not self-medication. Drinking because one cannot deal with the pain of life's problems is. Be careful to take prescription medication only as directed and do not mix it with alcohol.

In the therapy world, smoking is sometimes referred to as "slow suicide." In hypnotherapy classes, we were instructed to help move clients towards living a healthy, worthwhile life and away from wanting this slow suicide. Remember, you are modeling behavior for your children.

It is not worth giving your husband ammunition in a custody battle, by drinking or taking drugs. You do not know when a surprise drug test may be ordered by the court, if there are rumors of usage. You are teaching your children a crucial life skill when you deal with your problems in a constructive manner.

# 11

## Supporting Yourself with Supplements

### Bach Flower Remedies

*P*eople have shared stories of how Bach Flower Remedies! have made a difference in their lives. Dr. Bach was a physician (1886–1936) who had the modern thinking that "Our fears, our cares, our anxieties, and things like that, open the path to the invasion of illness." Dr. Bach utilized different flower essense combinations to get rid of mental and emotional stress. Current research has shown the link between stress and/or anger in bringing on heart attacks and strokes. These flower remedies are helpful in preventing a condition or disease. The remedies are also specific to certain anxieties.

For long term use during my divorce, I used Walnut, which is for a change in your life, such as a divorce, move, new job or loss of someone.

"The remedy gives constancy and protection from outside influences." It really did its job and I felt calmer and more in control during my divorce. I used this daily. One mother uses Walnut to help her deal with her son's divorce and said she feels more relaxed about it now.

Rescue Remedy is quick acting and used in acute situations, such as a court hearing. I literally used three to four drops a few minutes before I walked in the door for my collaborative divorce sessions. A few times, I excused myself during the middle and popped a few more drops in my mouth. Post-divorce, when we had a court hearing, Rescue Remedy was invaluable. I keep SLEEP Rescue Remedy in my nightstand and do three squirts if I wake up in the middle of the night.

One teacher told me that her college-age son was roaming around South America and she had been very anxious about the situation. There is even a flower remedy for when you are worried about your children, but they are not with you, so their fate is out of your hands. Wish I knew which one she took, because it worked.

White Chestnut is for those who cannot stop persistent thoughts, ideas or arguments entering their minds, making sleep and concentration more difficult. I am using this one now, post-divorce.

Willow is for those who suffered great adversity and feel that it was unfair. They are embittered and lose interest in previously enjoyable pursuits. One can see how well these remedies can benefit people going through divorce. Another good one is Olive, for those who have suffered much mentally or physically and feel that they have no more strength to deal with daily life. This one may be helpful for women coming out of an abusive marriage.

The above information can be found at the display area surrounding the bottles of Bach Flower Remedies in stores such as Pharmaca or Vitamin Cottage (natural grocers and herbalists). This information can also be obtained, by ordering online. A naturopath can offer assistance with choosing the best remedies for you.

Dr. Bach said that the thymus is particularly affected by the emotions of hate and envy. An under active-thymus depresses the immune system. Dr. Bach said that illness is "Disharmony and imbalance...between the soul and the mind."

There are specific remedies for children, which can aid yours through this transition. Many veterinarians recommend Rescue Remedy for animals, especially those who stress out when going to the clinic. I have sprayed this into cats' mouths during fights with good results (being careful not to get injured in the process). If your pets are moving into a new environment due to the divorce, check with your veterinarian to see if Rescue Remedy is right for them.

**Confused About What Supplements to Take for Stress or Heart?**

Red wine has been given a lot of press recently for protecting one's heart. Its extract is Resveratrol, an antioxidant which is also being studied for Alzheimer's, because it aids in breaking down amyloid plaque. Red Yeast Rice is indicated for lowering cholesterol, along with a healthy diet.

Studies indicate that Omega-3 protects the heart and decreases inflammation in the body. The Journal of Psychiatry is studying the use of Omega-3 for people with depression and other mental disorders. Another study advocates Omega-3 for kids with asthma, and my son was able to permanently get off an asthma medicine with regular usage. Remember, a good portion of your brain is made up of healthy fat, so these healthy fats in Omega-3 are useful for brain functioning and memory.

Another important supplement for stress is Holy Basil, which decreases cortisol levels. Cortisol is a stress hormone which causes increased heart rate, blood pressure and insomnia. Cortisol is responsible for the "flight or fight" response. In Indian Ayurvedic medicine, Holy Basil also has anti-mutagenic, and anti-inflammatory properties. This helped me to relax better and get to sleep quicker during my divorce, and I continue to take this fantastic supplement post-divorce.

High cortisol levels can cause headaches and aromatherapists often recommend Clary Sage essential oil to reduce this pain and relax muscles in the cranial-sacral areas. Lavender has a soothing effect on anxiety and comes in many forms, such as a facial spray or in a small bottle to roll on your temples and wrists. Scientists at Stanford University suggest calming the central nervous system by inhaling the fragrance of tangerine.

Bee pollen has vitamins, amino acids, trace minerals and enzymes. Milk thistle helps to promote healthy liver functioning and detoxification. This is particularly good if you have been eating more junk food, or have a glass too many with the girls.

B vitamins are marketed as the stress vitamins, because when your body in under stress, more are required. Lecithin granules contain phospholipids and help the brain in learning. I also take it for its aid in nerve functioning, since phospholipids are found in the brain tissue.

Co Enzyme Q10 is an element found in the mitochondria of cells, particularly those in the heart. It converts food into energy and diminishes free radicals. Skin care companies have added Q10 into their wide ranges of beauty products. I take it every day to promote healthy heart functioning.

Some busy mothers have commented that they and the kids do not consume enough green veggies. While it is preferable to eat more green vegetables, drinking them will do. There are several green powders that you can mix with water to fill this nutritional gap. Green Edge Powder or Perfect Green are two examples that contain all sorts of vegetables, grasses, seeds and seaweed to give your family a nutritional boost.

If you are not a breakfast person, or need a quick nutritional boost before leaving the house, here is a tip. Consume a protein powder mixed with milk, such as Spiru-tein. It contains trace elements, amino acids, chlorophyll, enzymes, apple pectin, vitamins and minerals. I do not take a multi-vitamin/mineral because of this drink and my bee pollen later in the day.

Verify whether your supplements have a single ingredient or are combinations. My Omega-3 is just that, but other brands have Resveratrol in them. Some Q10 capsules also contain Omega-3, listed in smaller print. You do not want to double up on some of these supplements by accident, as they can be costly. Check the labels carefully.

Stress and strong emotions can wreak havoc with your bowel functioning. A GI doctor gave me this tip: Take psyllium to regulate your GI tract, whether having diarrhea or constipation. For diarrhea, psyllium bulks up the stool, and for constipation, it helps you become more regular. Metamucil contains psyllium. I buy psyllium for less than a brand name one at Trader Joe's grocery store and it does not have additives. Check with your healthcare provider before adding supplements to your diet.

# 12

## Why Have Therapy?

Therapy helps you develop greater insight on various situations and handle relationships better. Therapy cannot make you instantly happy, but it can illuminate a path that leads you to have an easier time in life. Lucy Beresford states, in UK's *Psychologies Magazine*, that "Therapy won't work miracles, but it can do many other things. It can boost self-esteem, untangle emotional dilemmas, provide support during grief or trauma, facilitate the discovery of courage to face the world again after illness, divorce." A therapist can help someone who feels stuck in her life or at a crossroads, by enabling her to sort things out and get motivated for change.

In one case that I read about, an otherwise happily married couple could not agree on one issue and it was causing them emotional trauma. The therapist solved the problem in one session and it worked. The wife wanted fresh air at night and would open the bedroom window. The husband did not desire the fresh air blowing directly on him. The therapist asked detailed questions and came up with a plan. Open the bathroom window instead. The wife got fresh air and the husband did not have it blowing on him.

**Types of Therapy**

Some people wonder what type of questions they will be asked by a therapist. That depends upon the type of therapy your psychologist practices. For example, classical analysts (as in a Woody Allen film) will let you do most of the talking and may sit behind you. This type of therapy can take years. A therapist that does cognitive behavior therapy gives more advice and helps clients change thought patterns and expectations. Cognitive therapy is more concrete and works well with phobias, addictions and obsessive compulsive disorder. The cognitive psychologist may give an estimate for a specific number of sessions, since this is a much shorter type of therapy.

Humanistic therapy deals with your individual development as a person, rather than on a mental disorder. These therapists feel that events, such as abuse in childhood, interrupt the person's development, and they work with the client to fix the developmental process.

You do not have to tell your therapist your deepest, darkest secrets, but not doing so can impede your progress in therapy. What you withhold may be the crucial piece of information that needs to be addressed to improve your well-being. Some people are afraid they may become too dependent upon the therapist or even develop romantic feelings towards them. Transference is when you view your therapist as more of a parent or partner. It may be embarrassing, but bring it up, because this can happen in therapy, and therapists are especially trained on how to deal with this issue. Your therapist can work with the concept of transference to enable your other relationships to be more meaningful.

Often, at the beginning of therapy, your therapist will discuss how many sessions that he thinks you will need. Of course, this can be adjusted if you sail through and feel you have met your goals early. If more complex issues arise, then the amount of sessions will lengthen. Ultimately, you have the final say on when to stop the sessions. Success will be judged by noticing a difference in how you think and handle situations. This can be a very gradual process.

Group therapy is especially effective when it centers around a specific issue, such as grief or addictions. The other group members can help each other gain clarity and see that they are not the only one in that situation. The group leader may or may not be a psychologist. What is said in group therapy does not leave the room.

Hypnosis is one of the three natural altered states of the mind, with the other two being meditation and prayer. In hypnosis, the barrier between the conscious and subconscious minds opens. The subconscious is more receptive to suggestions for change and will only accept directions that are in your belief system. If you are against theft, then in hypnosis your subconscious mind would not accept the suggestion to embezzle or rob a bank. The subconscious mind runs the autonomic nervous system, so that is why hypnosis is such a valuable agent to instigate bodily change. The autonomic nervous system regulates breathing, blood pressure, heart rate, metabolism, cell changes, and so forth. Hypnotherapy helps with a plethora of conditions, such as insomnia, weight control, back pain, smoking cessation, anxiety, plus much more. Hypnotherapy delves back to the root of the problem and deals with the surrounding emotions, in order to release them, thereby promoting healing.

The subconscious mind is very literal. If your basic needs were not met as small child, it may conclude that you are "not worthy." This feeling of being "not worthy" can run your life, driving you to seek out people and situations that validate that you are "not worthy." Hypnosis is invaluable in changing these faulty self beliefs, and can sometimes make huge changes in only one session.

# 13

## Ways to Discover and Save Money

You will require money to pay your attorney's retainer and other divorce expenses. This chapter will help you reach that goal with lots of good ideas. When my husband left me, I lost my job and had no income for over a month, while the interim support was being determined. The bills still needed to be paid, so I had to discover ways to obtain instant cash from my belongings. My sons helped with thinking up ways to slash spending. I still had to give gifts and buy food, personal care products and so forth. I bought a house during my divorce, and required a chunk of cash for the down payment. This chapter gives detailed suggestions which were road tested by various women getting divorces or those who were on tight budgets.

A simple way to avoid high plumbing bills is to remove the clogs in drains with "Zip-It." This nifty gadget is a long piece of flexible plastic with small protuberances that grab hair easily. Even unskilled people like me can do it. I bought it at Ace Hardware for less than $10 and it has lasted four years so far. This "Zip-It" saves you from spending money on costly chemicals or natural remedies to unclog those drains.

**Gift-giving**

These girlfriends' tips for giving great Christmas or other occasion gifts will save you much money, with no big January bills. Go through your treasure and see what you can give to someone else who will appreciate them, particularly to family members. One grandfather gave his grandchild part of his coin collection. The child loved the old penny set, dating back to the 1800s. A grandmother gave her two grandsons old coins from her birth date in the 1920s. She is no longer here, so the boys really appreciated her thoughtfulness.

A niece or daughter who is a first time mother may treasure her grandmother's first edition Raggedy Ann books or other children's storybooks. Of course, add something new to the gift, but the major part would be antique baby china or books. People receive so much clothing at baby showers and the infant grows quickly, hardly wearing some outfits for very long. Family heirlooms last.

Do you have a chef in the family? One mother gave her chef-in-training son his great-grandmother's cookbook with her hand written notes. Also included in that gift was a copy of his preschool cookbook that she received as a present one year. A gift card to a local gourmet shop is a nice added touch.

Homemade goodies at the holidays are especially appreciated by teachers and overbooked, working mothers. Magazines have great ideas in this department. My tip is to go to a charity shop and pick up a lovely platter or plate for a dollar or two and present your yummy treats on these. Yes, I have seen antique ones at this price, too.

A great source of presents is your jewelry collection. Pare it down and give some turquoise necklaces and bracelets to a fan of Native American jewelry. For a lover of glass beads, part with one of your necklaces from Venice. You get the idea, so be creative and save a wad of cash.

Start drawing names for a Christmas gift exchange, so each kid buys something for one cousin and you are not purchasing twenty toys for nieces and nephews. Maybe just the kids can participate in the gift exchanges. One family could give a group gift to another family, such as yummy treats and a popular DVD. Your family members may want to limit gifts, but are afraid to be the ones who initially bring up the idea. Ask them how they feel about drawing another's name for a more limited gift exchange. I read how three sisters put a limit of around $15 for each other's birthday gifts. The competition is so fierce, you would think it was a blood sport. The ladies find fabulous gifts on the cheap when traveling, at clearance sales, etc., but all manage to give incredible presents on that budget.

Here is a way to have no debts after Christmas, with holiday gift-giving. Layaway. Yes, layaway is back in fashion in these trying economic times. K-Mart does layaway as well as a high-end local consignment shop. This way you can start selecting gifts and making your payments in affordable increments in advance. Be sure to examine your budget to determine how much you can spend on presents, so that the payments will be completed before Christmas. This can enable you to curtail those last minute-impulse purchases so you do not have to pay bills in January.

Girlfriends have steered me towards finding great holiday presents in thrift shops or jumble sales. People donate new items, sometimes still in their original boxes, to these places. It may be because these items are not their cup of tea, or they may be the contents of a deceased family member's estate. Inspect clothes to see if anything in someone's size still has the tags on it. Check out household goods for new linens, etc., still in their wrappers. People donate new books when they get duplicates. I have found some wonderful CDs still in cellophane. Also, seek out the vintage toys or book selections for your gift list.

School or church jumble sales have unique selections, brought together for one day's hunting. I found an unopened Ravensburger puzzle, which I later sold online. At that same school sale, I bought four 1920s French art magazines, which I sold.

My big tip is to check out charity shops when traveling, to purchase locally made products at a fraction of the usual cost. Oxfam is a wonderful charity, whose UK shops are treasure troves. I did a good bit of shopping at one when on a nurses' conference in St. Andrews, Scotland. It was centrally located and sold locally made vases and other handicrafts, which were brand new.

## How to Get Money From Your Possessions

Check your jewelry box and other places around your house for broken chains, old class rings and jewelry which you no longer like or wear. You may find some beat up sterling silverware and utensils. Take them to your local metal/coin shop to get instant cash. Local coin shops want your repeat business, and I found mine to be honest and fair. Some jewelry stores can melt down the metals and extract the stones from some pieces and sell them both. I have heard mixed reviews about the places where you mail in your jewelry or companies coming to town for one day to purchase your goods. Old family pieces, which are tarnished or just 10 karat gold, can also be sold. If the item is gold or silver-plated, then it is not accepted at my local metal shop. Even relatives' gold teeth fillings can be sold. A few dollars here and there add up quickly.

Go to your local consignment store to sell higher quality jewelry. Some may buy your pieces outright. You would be surprised what your great aunt's broach will fetch. Unique or antique jewelry boxes can do well also. Polish your jewelry and silver items before taking them to a consignment shop.

Another avenue is to sell your jewelry online. Brand names do better than generic pieces, because buyers often look up items by brands, such as Tiffany or Zales. If you do not want to do online sales yourself, then take them to a local business that puts items online for a percentage of the sale. I have even gotten decent prices selling my jewelry at garage sales, particularly if I put an ad in the paper stating that I had bracelets and rings to sell. For very unique pieces, some people put an ad in the classifieds with a photograph.

Instead of selling extra nice coffee table books or gift-type ones at your garage sale, make a lot more by taking them to a used book dealer. Over the last several years, I have made several hundred dollars extra by doing just this. Do you have any childhood books, which are not first editions, but are early ones? I sold mine at a local bookstore when they did not sell online. Art books, classics and ones with unique subjects do well at these stores. I have even called the owner of the used bookstore from garage sales and charity shops to see if some books are worth purchasing and selling to him at a small profit. He is very kind about that since we have done a lot of business together. Sometimes you can sell a signed, first edition online.

You can get a tax write off if you donate books to charities or schools. I donate animal-themed books to the animal shelter thrift shop.

Look through your old toys and games. I sold my Nancy Drew game for $65 online and other ones for a little less. My gently used Coach handbags have fetched a modest price. People collect figurines. Do an inventory of items that you can live without and check their prices online. If you really do love a plate and it is only selling for $15, it is better to keep it. Use the Internet to get an up to the minute guide for pricing, even if you are taking items to a consignment shop.

I have sold some paintings through a local art dealer and made ten times my initial investment. I bought these through a few estate sales that were not run by a professional company, but directly from the buyer. I sold several paintings that I bought at charity auctions for two to three times the original price. Most of these paintings were several hundred dollars to just over a thousand.

Tips for saving money around your house. To avoid paying for extra electricity that you're not currently using, unplug appliances, phone chargers and so forth. Many people are unaware that electricity still goes from the wall to your appliance, even when it is turned off. When my coffee maker is turned off, there still is a light on, unless it is unplugged. Tell your kids to unplug the toaster when they are done using it. This is the reason that some kittens are injured, because they feel the electrical current going through the electrical cord and then play with the cord. Check with your utility company to see if the rates are cheaper at certain non-peak times and do your washing then. Put your computer, printer and other gadgets on a power strip with an off switch. Turn it off when not in use, especially at bedtime. I fine my older son a dollar per night if he leaves the power strip on, after being on his computer. So far, I only had to collect this fee once.

Do not automatically turn on a light when you enter a room, such as a bathroom, if you can get enough light through a window to brush your teeth. You will increase the value of your house if you add several sky lights, and you may be eligible for an energy saving tax write off. Good places for these would be in your kitchen or over your bathroom countertop.

When you are brushing your teeth, turn off the water, unless you are actually rinsing off your toothbrush. My sons scoop up the water from their baths or showers to water plants. If you visit the Middle Eastern countries, such as Jordan, you can see how precious water really is. I was told in Jordan that future wars will be over water rights and restrictions. Some people collect rain water in barrels and water their gardens from this. These barrels have spigots to which one can attach a hose.

When you buy gas, make sure to get every drop. Do not disconnect the gas hose form your car immediately. Rather, wait a moment and confirm that there are not any drops left. I fill up my car to almost full to make sure that my tank has room for those remaining drops. Gas is more condensed when the weather is colder, so fill up your tank in the morning.

For another tip on saving money on gas, UPS recently came up with having their drivers deliver packages by only making right turns. The drivers' routes were configured by plotting out a course with these right turns, stating that money will be saved on gas. Is this true? The "Myth Busters" TV show decided to disprove or prove this interesting hypothesis. They had the same route with random turns and then with just right ones. "Myth Busters" even stopped to deliver packages at the same points, just as UPS would. It was significantly better, saving time as well as gas, when making only right turns. Idling wasted much time when waiting to make left turns. In conclusion, plan your errands by charting a course of right turns.

## Household Hints

In the kitchen, get the most out of your trash liners. When you have messy garbage, such as peelings or egg shells, put them inside a container in the trash bin, such as an empty cereal box. This way, you can reuse liners instead of throwing them away each time when you empty the garbage. Plastic bags from store purchases can be used to line small trash cans.

Egg shells can go in the soil for plants, giving them extra nutrients. Buy vegetable broth or a vegetable soup in a box to use as a base, then put any leftover vegetables in this. You can puree this soup, or leave it chunky.

Reuse the wax paper bags inside cereal boxes. Shake out any crumbs and use these to put cold cuts in, and to put over opened food in the freezer. When I buy rolls or scones, I use the bags from a cereal box for these baked goods. Bouquets of flowers in the grocery stores have pretty, colorful paper under the cellophane wrapper. Let this air dry and cut it up to wrap smaller presents.

Remember to use tissue paper from shoe boxes and other purchases to wrap Christmas stocking stuffers. Save ribbons and the metallic cords from chocolate boxes to reuse for tiny gifts.

Here are a few tips about cleaning for low or no cost. Use a recycled spray bottle with 1/3 bleach to 2/3 water to spray on counters or floors. I use this around the shower and window sills to prevent mildew. Some people prefer to use hydrogen peroxide instead of bleach. After using a cotton square with toner for my face, I use it to clean around the sink area, particularly if there are traces of toothpaste or soap scum. My vanity area is sparking, with no cost for spot cleanups. If you have marble or granite counter tops, you may just want to clean the sink area with the used toner pad.

After taking a shower, when the mirror is still steamy, take a cloth or paper towel and take advantage of free steam power to wipe off spots from the mirror. When traveling, use the shampoo in the hotel to clean your clothes, without spending money to tote along special fabric wash. My clothes have always done well with this and I avoid expensive laundering charges.

Use the cotton that is in vitamin or supplement bottles to remove makeup. I can get three uses out of it, by dividing that one piece of cotton. If we use paper napkins, I reuse them to clean up spots on my floors.

## Look Like a Goddess, Spend Like Scrooge

Some great skin products are at least 1/2 to 2/3 of the department or specialty store price, such as the Boots Botanics line, which can be found at Target. Boots is a pharmaceutical store chain originating in the UK, which carries natural, healthy products. My favorite is Boots Botanics organic body oil which sells for around $10 which is certified organic by Kew Gardens in London. It is chock full of plant nutrition for your skin and a little goes a long way. I first read about this product in British magazines and they raved about how it out-performs more expensive brands. The body lotion has the same high quality ingredients. During my divorce, my sons commented on how I was developing worry lines on my face, particularly my forehead. I used Boots "Eye and Lip Correction Serum" and erased these lines by the time my divorce was over. When they start creeping back, it's because I have been lax using it, so I restart again. Boots "Cold Cream" with rose is fantastic for removing make up. I use it early evening to quicken my bedtime routine, and my face stays hydrated until I wash it much later. "Soothing Eye Make up Remover" from the Botanics line contains "Iceland Moss." In the morning "Organic Face Rosewater Toner" is used after washing your face. At night, I sometimes use "Radiance Renewal Night Serum." I use the "Organic Face Super Balm" as the top layer before suncream. Just the tiniest dab will do. These products are so reasonable, many under $10.

Trader Joe's has some well performing lotions and body oils, packed full of nutrients without preservatives, dyes and other chemicals. Their jojoba body oil is around $7, lovely lavender body oil is $5 and the body cream is a bargain for around $4. Their lavender or grapefruit $6 body scrubs work well, but do leave the tub a bit slick. Another reasonable body lotion available in many places is Swiss St. Ives, for around $5.

A money saver is to use your favorite brand's body butter, instead of designated hand lotion, with similar results. My body butter is eight ounces and the hand lotion is 1.5 ounces at almost the same price. I purchase a hand lotion only to tote around in my purse or travel bag.

There is more luxe for less. Lumene from Finland is affordable, especially when CVS Pharmacy has a buy one and get the second for half off. Lumene line's products range from $5 to $30 and has ingredients such as Arctic cloudberry, cranberry, and Vitamin C. I use the "Energy Cocktail Intensive Serum" first in the morning, which has the consistency of water. One squirt does my whole face, so it is very economical. "Time Freeze Instant Lift Serum" is keeping my neck taut. "Rejuvenating Instant Serum" goes on next and really wakes me up. Remember that skin absorbs medicines and chemicals, so make sure you use high quality products such as the ones mentioned above.

Have baby soft feet using Vermont's "Bag Balm," which has been produced for over 100 years. This ten ounce tin of ointment costs around $9 and a tiny bit is all that is needed to heal dry, cracked heels. I rub it on my feet after I get in bed and wake up with silky skin. This is sold in Vermont's country stores or at Walgreen's.

I used to buy several French brands of foundation, but discovered Boots No.7 Foundation works better than any of them for me. What a surprise to discover that it is made in France. This foundation is around $15 at Target and was, or still is, the world's leading seller. This Boots brand blush is more effective than the French one that I previously used. Boots lip gloss stays on better than the French one I used to use, at a fraction of the cost. You can look like a goddess with Boots cosmetics.

Friends have tried Burt's Bees products and also rate them with high marks. You can buy natural skincare and cosmetics, for great prices, but do check the labels.

Farmer's and Flea markets have natural lotions, lavender sachets and other goodies made with locally grown herbs and plants. Their prices are lower, without having a store's overhead. These are fresh, without preservatives, so you may want to use them soon after purchasing. These are unique, but reasonable to give as girlfriend gifts.

# 14

## Divorce Negotiations

You may want to have the children remain on your husband's insurance plan as part of the support package. See if this coverage can be extended through college or at least until they are twenty-one. Have your lawyer state that the children's insurance plan cannot be changed without your consent. This became important post-divorce for me. The plan that my ex has includes one doctor visit a year without co-pays, plus pays for part of medications. He wanted to change it to a plan with co-pays, which meant I would be trying to collect what is due me more often. I vetoed this idea. Your spouse will be unable to change to an inferior health plan, or one with a higher deductible or co-pays.

During your divorce, any life insurance policies may have to be cashed in and used as an asset to be divided. My husband's life insurance policy was bought and paid for during our marriage and netted $58,000. This money went into the community asset pot, which was used for collaborative fees and to renovate our house for resale, with the remainder split between us. Whoever is paying child support could be mandated to take out a new life insurance policy in at least the amount that covers future alimony and child support. Make sure you are listed as a beneficiary and get a copy of this at least once a year.

Alimony is taxable income for you and child support is not taxed. Your ex gets a tax break with alimony, but does not get any with child support. One woman with small children opted to forego alimony and take all her money as child support, so she did not have to pay any taxes on it. My attorney suggested taking less child support for me, since I had older children and to take a much larger alimony. I do have to pay more taxes, but I will be receiving alimony a bit longer after my child support ends.

States base alimony on how long you have been married. In my particular state, being married twenty years seems to be the magic number for a larger alimony. There is a formula which incorporates time married, how many children, the time spent at the parent's house who is receiving child support (such as 50/50), plus the amount of both people's wages. This is how the amount of child support/alimony is calculated in my region of the USA. My attorney stipulated that my alimony continues until the specified ending date, with no pre-payment. Have it put in the decree that you continue to receive alimony whether or not you remarry or cohabitate. Occasionally, people take the settlement in one huge, lump sum, as some celebrities opt to do, rather than in monthly payments. This is particularly good if you feel that your ex would disappear, or somehow would not have the money or make the payments down the road. You could invest the money yourself, which then could provide you with a monthly income.

There is modifiable and non-modifiable alimony, with pros and cons to both. My husband wanted to revisit the alimony issue two years after our divorce, and the last thing I wanted to do was to go through the whole thing again. I went the non-modifiable route, with no changes allowed in the amount of my alimony, except if he declared bankruptcy. If your ex's income takes a nose dive post-divorce, but he does not declare bankruptcy, he is still responsible for the same amount of alimony. However, if it looks like he will be getting a prestigious promotion, or is starting to become a well-known author, you may want modifiable, so you can take him to court for an increase in alimony and child support.

In cases where the woman out-earns the man, or if he was a stay-at-home father, then she may be ordered to pay alimony. This happened to actress Jane Seymour, and she had some strong words for the press regarding this issue. A divorced female news show host echoed this same sentiment. Paying spousal support comes as a shock to many women, particularly if they were doing the bulk of home and child care, along with bringing home the bacon.

The new trend in my state is for the husband to pay a higher amount of alimony, for a shorter time period, usually five to six years. I opted for this and used it to pay off my mortgage. I saved money by not paying my previous average of $1,700 per year in mortgage interest. I have one son in college, so the extra amount of alimony is handy now. I usually put what I would have paid in mortgage payments into an investment account, so I will have a little nest egg when my alimony ends. The down side to this alimony arrangement is that the safety net is gone – no more divorce income for life. With this method, you really have to be disciplined and sock some money away for later years.

I highly recommend that you have the alimony/support check automatically deposited into your bank account through your former spouse's financial institution. I cannot emphasize enough all the problems down the road that this protocol will prevent. No "the check must have gotten lost in the mail" or having to contact your ex, to see why a check is late. Your ex is physically not involved with your monthly check; the two financial institutions are instead. Much easier.

# 15

## Dividing Assets

While the divorce financial adviser will do an excellent job valuing assets and determining how much each spouse receives, it is up to you to decide what particular assets you want. It is prudent to diversify them. For example, if you want the $200,000 house, you will have to give up $100,000 in assets to your spouse. If your husband chooses to receive his half from a money market account, and the housing market crashes, your half of the value of the house could be a lot less than $100,000. If, in a year, it is only valued at $140,000, your share is really only $70,000. However, at least you have a place to live with the least disturbance for the children.

Remember to factor in future interest payments when dividing up assets. For example, If your husband gets $200,000 cash or assets up front and you opt to wait until something sells to get yours, then you have lost potential interest. If your husband will give you a $200,000 piece of property in a year's time, the annual interest @ 3% is $6,000. That is $6,000 you would lose in delaying the receipt of this asset, so that has to be factored into the division when settling.

Betsy really wanted their house, even though it was larger than she needed. She had a sentimental attachment to it, so fought hard to get it in their divorce, and it became her main received asset. There was still a mortgage on it, plus other expenses, like a high property tax, insurance and maintenance. It seemed like most of her salary was going for the house upkeep. Sometimes it may be better to sell the house, pay off the mortgage and split the difference. Betsy could have found a smaller and cheaper place, plus have had a little nest egg. Other options are to get a roommate or have a home-based business, if possible. There is a tax-break for a home-based business, such as having your office there, where you see clients. Three therapists that I know of have converted their garages into client therapy rooms.

If your husband applied for a patent or wrote a book while still married, then you have negotiating rights for future payments. If you worked and helped put your husband through grad school, then see if you can get more future earnings or some type of payback.

Make sure your lawyer and financial adviser are aware of other perks, such as his frequent flier miles, or hotel points, which could be divided or traded for other assets. If he wants to keep your joint country club or golf membership, check what its value is it now. Call the country club yourself and talk with the membership department to find out what it is worth or what it would cost to buy it now.

If your parents paid a credit card bill for your husband, as my mother did, find that record. She was able to get her $6,800 back in the divorce, because she had the canceled check showing that she directly paid his Mastercard bill one month. If your parents loaned you both some money, make sure they are paid back first, before assets are divided.

This is particularly important if your parents helped you with a down payment or helped with any principle or mortgage payments. Get documentation. Elena's mother helped a couple buy their first house, so her name was also on the deed. This was tremendous help in her daughter's divorce. The bank had changed hands and the financial officer had retired, so they did not have good documentation for the mother's share of the house. The lawyers were going to give the couple and the wife's mother each a one third share of the house. By chance, the wife ran into the retired bank financial officer during the divorce and quickly called her lawyer's paralegal from the grocery store and got this woman on the phone. So, instead of buying her husband out for a one third share, it was now only one sixth. Any records from your parents can assist in divvying up assets when they have contributed some of the payments.

If any big ticket items were a personal gift to you from your parents, have them put that in writing to your attorney. My mother had to do this, so a Waterford chandelier and other items were not counted as joint assets in my divorce. This would be particularly important in the case of a car or an expensive piece of artwork given as a gift to you personally from your family.

Unfortunately, if money or stock gifts received from your family were merged into a joint account, then it is joint property in a divorce. It is worthwhile to check into receiving some of his retirement as part of your divorce package. You may want to hire your own financial adviser to look over the assets to be divided. That way you will get what is best for your personal financial interests.

Here are three pitfalls to avoid when splitting an income together, post-divorce. Both Terri and her husband wanted the quarterly income from a joint investment, which netted $2,000 to $10,000 each quarter. Since it varied so much, it was too hard to assign it to either spouse. The income was derived from a piece of medical equipment at the hospital, which could last for two to fifteen more years. The financial adviser told the husband to check and see if the investment could be divided into two, so that each spouse independently owned a share. The mistake came when the husband later said "not possible." No one investigated whether the husband had really checked, or if the financial adviser could have devised a way to implement a split by working with the company directly. Secondly, if the investment truly could not be split, then the person originally writing the check should have been mandated to write each spouse an equal amount instead of just one check to the husband. Thirdly, the wife's attorney made the error of not inserting into the decree that the wife would receive half of the GROSS amount. At least Terri insisted that a photo copy of the original check be sent with her check.

The ex took out $2,700 in "expenses" from her check, because his lawyer argued that Terri only received the NET. After expensive legal bills, Terri received the half of the GROSS amount and the check in a timely manner. Inserting "gross" is important, so your ex cannot try and give you less than your fair share.

During your divorce, joint accounts and credit cards should be closed. Each spouse should have a credit card in his or her name to prevent future liability issues. The balance on our two credit cards was completely paid off before we received any assets. Post-divorce, we each started with a clean slate.

Ask to claim the children as dependents on your tax form. My attorney calculated that my husband would only save about $35 per child, due to his higher tax bracket. However, if I claimed the boys, I would save a few hundred dollars each, because of my much lower one. My husband's lawyer readily agreed that it made more sense for me to take this deduction post-divorce.

# 16

## Dividing Personal Property

My attorney said that couples have split millions of dollars in assets calmly, but divorces have nearly derailed while trying to divide personal property. This subject is a minefield, so my attorney does it at the very end of the divorce process. Unfortunately, my sons and I had to move out of the family house, because it had to be renovated for resale during our divorce, so we had to deal with this issue earlier than we would have preferred.

There are different ways to approach this, but often the spouse still in the house does the household inventory. Items may be listed with a value, after the more expensive ones are professionally appraised. Other times, just the items are listed without any values and the spouses each take similar items in the different categories. You might each take a painting by the same artist, or nearly identical antiques. If you are not sure what particular artwork to request, consider hiring your own art appraiser to give you some guidance.

Other spouses each have one color of stickers and take turns putting them on desired objects. They flip a coin to see who goes first. There is give and take with this process. Some attorneys have their clients make three separate lists: What you really want, what you would like and what you do not particularly care about. If your spouse is vindictive, this can be the most trying and tedious part of the whole divorce. To be vindictive, Nina's husband pointedly left gifts that she and his sons gave him. Nina had the last laugh, when a collector pair of mugs sold for $175 on e-Bay and his books fetched $155 at a used book shop. She sold some of his other things and waited until the divorce was final, and then got a tax write-off for the rest.

I put my children's outgrown clothes, toys and my things in my mother's garage and also waited until after the divorce to take them to charity shops so I could claim the tax-write off on my next year's tax form. If you do this during your divorce, then you split the tax write-off on your last married tax form that is filed with your husband. If you are divorcing in November or December, then you will sign the divorce papers, but it will not be filed with the court until January 2nd. Otherwise, you would be filing two tax returns for the same year, one married and one single. On January 2nd, you start off the tax year as single.

A regret that Kelly has is that she did not take much personal property when leaving with her two children. She left most of their toys, clothes and her own artwork (she's a painter) behind. Since Kelly took the kids across the state line erroneously, she lost her bargaining power and gave up most of her personal property in order to avoid more legal entanglements. A parent is not allowed to take a child across the state line without permission from or notification to the other parent. This is to prevent parental kidnapping or moving across country with the kids.

Tonya moved away from her family and friends in Fresno to live in Reno with her new husband. Things were great until they had kids. Her husband refused to change or cut down on his travel or work hours and saw very little of Tonya and their offspring. They divorced, and Tonya could not move with the kids back to Fresno, or even go for a long weekend without her husband's permission, as per the divorce decree.

In another case where the two sons had no contact with their father, their mother only had to notify the court monitor of the trip date and itinerary. The court monitor then sends these details via email to the father. It is easier when these issues are considered pre-marriage, and some couples address them in a pre-nup agreement. Definitely work out these issues during a divorce, so there are not acrimonious court battles afterward.

Other women said they wished that they had hired detectives to catch their husbands having affairs. These women felt that they would have had firmer footholds during their divorces and would have possibly gotten more property.

In my case, jewelry and trinkets were exempt from the inventory and we each got to keep our own. I owned sterling silver jewelry and my husband had mainly 18k gold, but I went along with this just to move through it all more quickly and move out of the house.

Lump his gifts and heirlooms from his relatives and his friends (including wedding presents) in one category, and do the same for you. You each would get your category as personal property. Some women already removed valuable and sentimental heirlooms from their homes during their turbulent marriages and gave them to a family member to store for safekeeping.

Any furniture, art or personal effects, that we each brought into the marriage remained ours in the personal property division. I clearly put this on the household inventory and marked the appropriate name by it. This was not up for negotiation.

The sheriff's department will send a deputy to be present, while your husband removes his allowed items, if notified ahead of time. A better option for me was to have my attorney's paralegal present the entire time that my husband packed up and moved his designated goods out of our house. She had a list of the inventory and kept him on track. I did not have to worry that something not on his list would be taken either on purpose or by accident.

If you have a friendly relationship with your husband, maybe just the two of you can get his stuff packed and out of the house. A few times, when my husband wanted this or that, I would leave it on the front porch at a designated time for pick up. This arrangement was done through my attorney.

A few couples I know felt that the division of personal property was taking up too much time with lawyers (more expensive). They met at coffee houses and got the inventory done and the division agreed upon during one sitting.

In Nina's case, her husband was vindictive and wanted to get everything. She soon realized that it takes two to have a battle and decided not to participate. She backed off and said, "These are the few things that I insist upon. Take the rest." The rest did not seem so interesting to her husband after that, so he also backed down a bit. Nina got more than she anticipated and was glad that she decided "not to get dirty rolling around in the mud with pigs." What also helped is that they owned a business together, and the financial adviser stepped in and told Nina's husband that since he wanted so much from the house, that Nina would get a lot of the artwork and personal property from their business. Her husband wanted the place of business to look the same, so he left most of the household goods for Nina. In situations like this one, when your husband and his lawyer see that you are not going to lock horns in battle, then they can become more reasonable. It takes at least two people to have a fight.

Pets may be divided up like personal property, with whomever you brought into the marriage remaining with you. Our cats have close ties with each other and particular friendships within the group. My feline-loving attorney stated that the cats needed to stay together as a unit. No one said anything and I held my breath, since I was the one who always took care of them. My attorney announced that they would remain with me and quickly moved on to the next topic.

I have heard about cases where the dog goes with the children when they have visitation with their fathers. Be creative. Sometimes animal custody can be the main sticky point with a divorce.

Benny is on good terms with his ex and house sits when she and her partner go on vacation. Benny is happy to spend time with his former dog and this situation benefits everyone. He also housesits for a few other friends to get his "dog fix."

Take the high road in divorce. Do not be like the couple in the 1989 movie, "War of the Roses" (Kathleen Turner and Michael Douglas) who did not take the high road and fought to the bitter end. Nobody won and the results were deadly. It is better to get through a divorce with one's sanity intact than to get into a knock-out battle. Two of my friends wanted out of their marriages and left with few community possessions. They both said that china and other goods were not worth the time and emotional burden it would take if they fought over them. Consequently, their divorces were both quick, and these people got nice china, artwork and houses in their subsequent marriages. Plus, the new pieces did not carry the memories of the last relationship.

# 17

## Decluttering and Letting Go

This is the time to go through your possessions and see what you can let go. Items that were significant in your marriage enable you to stay attached to your former spouse. If you kept the marital home in your divorce, then perhaps it is time to donate or sell some items and start anew. Catherine Ponder states in her book, *Open Your Mind to Prosperity*, that to achieve prosperity, "You must get rid of what you don't want to make the way for what you do want. " If your house is bursting at the seams with too many things, then you do not have room for more special ones to come into your life.

Australian comedian, Corrine Grants, tells about being a hoarder and the misery it caused in her book *Lessons in Letting Go: Confessions of a Hoarder*. Ms. Grant said that she hoarded under the mistaken idea that holding onto all of her things would protect her from feelings of guilt and regret. When she got past this, then she was ready to let go and clear up her junk.

A divorced family member of mine could not get past anger and other strong emotions post-divorce and held onto her possessions, accumulating more along the way. It was as if she thought her things were forming a protective cocoon around her. Being in her house was claustrophobic.

Ms. Grant has these tips for us. Figure out why you are holding on to too much stuff. Once you figure out what emotions are causing the hoarding, then it is easier to let go. Clear away the less painful and insignificant items first. Gain momentum before tackling the bigger, more important stuff. Just keep steadily working on it and do not set up nearly impossible time tables to accomplish this task. I just told myself to clear out and sort one large box every week. Once you have this momentum going, you may surprise yourself and do more. It is like beginning an exercise program, with just walking a short loop first to get started.

Keep just one article that reminds you of an event, not a trunk full. Do not throw out items in anger to get back at someone. If you cannot get started, ask a friend or a specialist to help you begin. Your pal does not have the same emotional attachment as you, and can see items in a more objective manner.

When you buy something new, that means something has to go out of your house. I have read that many women also apply this to clothes. If getting started is too daunting, then take photos to keep, and later get rid of the actual object.

## 18

## Legal Entanglements Post-Divorce

The next section is about legal entanglement issues that can affect you post-divorce. My first post-divorce hearing was approximately one year after my divorce was finalized. I was blindsided by the realization that our partnership had not ended by divorce, and that my former spouse was unable to move on. It was as if by taking me to court over the next few years, my ex could stay attached. The other part is that he represented himself for most of the hearings, so he had no legal fees, while mine added up quickly. Several different post-divorce experiences are shared to give insight on what may occur, no matter how well written your divorce decree is.

If you did not put in your divorce decree that spouses cannot contact the child protective services directly, then there could be a nasty surprise. Children's Protective Services are required to check out complaints, no matter how bogus. The problem is that the initial complaint may be lame, but while doing an inspection, other issues might emerge. You can be cited for having too many cats and not enough litter boxes. If a child comes into a parent's room at night to sleep after experiencing nightmares, that can be viewed as pathological. If you are moving and have boxes and piles of stuff everywhere, this constitutes a lack of space and untidy living conditions. Child Protective Services looks at exactly what is (messy house) and not what is happening in the near future (moving next week). These examples are actual cases. It is better to be prepared for what your ex may throw at you and prevent trouble by keeping your house clean and clutter at bay.

Another jarring surprise is having your ex get court papers delivered to your house via the police. It amps up the shock when a teenager answers the door and the policemen ask him for your phone number or your work address. You may receive a "Protection from Domestic Abuse," which is stating that you committed slander by making disparaging comments which could damage his reputation or social standing in the community. Also, the complaint may contain statements saying that you made false allegations regarding him to the children. These papers may be accompanied by "Temporary Order of

Protection and Order to Appear." Get an attorney immediately. If you did a collaborative divorce, your attorney may not be able to represent you in this situation, but she can certainly get you to another one. Your attorney may work with your ex's attorney to avoid a court hearing and draft a court document called a "Stipulated Order." Both former spouses agree not to talk about each other and to stay away from each other's residences and job sites. This way it is not one-sided, but the document entered in court is "Petitioner and Respondent" (not vs.) and pertains to both people. If you can avoid going to court, then do so. Court is emotionally draining and costly.

An ex spouse can file a "Motion for Order to Show Cause" on a specific issue, such as visitation. For example, there may have been child complaints regarding visitation which are now being modified. You are told by an official person, such as the court monitor, that visitation is being suspended and not to send your child to visitation until further notice. The father may file a motion in court accusing you of interfering with visitation. This is not a do-it-yourself project, so hire an attorney. Give your lawyer all the documentation, including emails, so that she can talk to the necessary people, including the therapist and court monitor. She will then file a motion with the court to quash (cancel) the hearing due to supporting documentation, which shows that you did as you were told regarding visitation (i.e., not sending your child).

Women like to connect with others and share bits of their lives that correlate with what another person is experiencing. Be careful, because that can backfire. Tammy is a newly divorced mom with two kids in high school. Alice is also a divorced mother of two, who has a daughter in Tammy's son's class. Both women have been acquaintances for years. The daughter helped Tammy's son deal with his parents' recent divorce and gave him advice. At a church festival, Tammy briefly thanked Alice for having such a wonderful daughter who was able to help her son cope with his parents' situation. This inspired Alice to unburden herself about her former husband: his viewpoints, faults, lack of monetary support and more custody/divorce issues. Tammy mainly listened and connected with her by sharing a few parallel experiences. Tammy was glad to be an ear for this poor woman's post-divorce woes.

Tammy was soon in shock when she received a court summons for slander against her ex, and Alice was his main witness. Alice's family also knew Tammy's ex, and Alice evidently revealed Tammy's few comments to him.

When Tammy was summoned to court by her ex-husband, she had another valuable lesson to learn. The judge looked vaguely familiar, but Tammy could not remember why. This judge limited Tammy's attorney to making only a few statements, and would always rule in her ex's favor. Tammy's attorney was quite flabbergasted by the judge's behavior and ordered transcripts of the court proceedings to verify this issue. Tammy started telling people about this particular judge to see if anyone else had had the same experience. One acquaintance was floored and said, "He cannot be your judge because he is a buddy of your ex." It turned out that Tammy had met the judge when still married, and had witnessed various interactions between these two men. She notified her attorney who filed for a hearing to have this judge recuse (dismiss) himself from any future court hearings. The judge did recuse himself, although was very defensive about his socializing with Tammy's ex. If you feel that you or your spouse have previously met your judge, do some research to verify that he and your ex are not lodge brothers, college alumni or in some other social situation together.

Post-divorce, only confide very personal information to just a few close pals who will not divulge anything you reveal to anyone, including their spouses. If you cannot be sure, then do your unburdening to a professional or to a support group. Tell your mother things only if she is not a blabbermouth. I again emphasize my attorney's advice; "Be careful what you say, because it can bite you in the butt."

# 19

## Self-respect

*"No one can make you feel inferior without your consent."*

— *Eleanor Roosevelt*

Self-respect can impact your whole family. One mother literally stood next to the table, at least when there were guests present, and waited on everyone hand and foot. I was uncomfortable that she really was not eating with us, but rather, acted like a waitress.

Sometimes we do not realize how others treat us greatly impacts our children.

Lonnie has two children, a girl and a boy. Her husband takes business trips around the globe, yet Lonnie has yet to go on one. Her husband takes their two children, usually individually on these jaunts. Last summer, he took their son to Europe for a month, hitting some wonderful capital cities. His excuse to the family was that he could not afford to take his wife along, too. What message does that give to their children? That wives are not important? That Lonnie's wishes and needs are much lower on the priority list? She has not taken business trips with me overseas either, (although we have the same college degree), because she did not want the kids, house and dog to be a burden on her husband. My concern is that when her son weds, that he will model his marriage on what he observed with his parents. Will their son feel that he is the most important person in the marriage, instead of it being a true partnership? Will the twenty-two-year-old daughter be a doormat for her husband? That would greatly impact her happiness.

Yes, I am guilty of this as well. Before my divorce, my husband would belittle me or put me down in front of our sons. Sometimes I would tell him that it was inappropriate behavior, but there were plenty of times that I kept mum, or addressed it in private. My sons began modeling their father's behavior. The point is that my sons started treating me as I allowed their father to treat me.

After our divorce, our sons only lived with me, but had some daytime visitation with their father. We addressed how to be respectful and have a loving relationship with future wives. Now I say, "Nope, I cannot drive you there. I am going to have a pedicure now." I am just as important as my children.

Some women "run away" once a year for a girlfriend's weekend trip to a spa or city escape. Not only does this recharge their batteries, but it lets the families know that friendships and personal pursuits are valued. So, to help ensure that your children have healthy marriages and are respectful to all others, demand that you are shown the respect that is rightfully yours. Do it for your kids, even if you feel you cannot demand it for yourself.

# 20

## Not Failure, Only Feedback

When something does not work out as anticipated, it can be considered a form of feedback. Sometimes what seems like a colossal mistake turns out to be an indicator that you are actually on the right path. For example, a pharmaceutical company did a study for an anti-hypertensive medication. The results were so dismal that the company decided to cut its losses and end the study early. The medication failed miserably and did not even come close to achieving the desired result. The company told the study participants to return the unused doses. Many men refused to turn in the left over pills to the pharmaceutical company. After much probing, the company discovered the surprising reason why. Pfizer later named those little blue pills of the former failed drug, Viagra, and history was made.

Some people have said that when they lost their jobs, it seemed like the end of the world. The future looked bleak and they felt like failures. Only later did they realize that this was a gift, feedback that something much better was ready to happen. A few used severance pay to re-train for different jobs, which worked out wonderfully, increasing family time and decreasing stress. Others used the opportunity to retire from the "rat race" and live a more simple lifestyle, choosing to do artistic work or grow an herb garden.

One couple was having difficulty making ends meet selling homemade chocolates in their rural shop. Instead of seeing this as failure, they saw it as feedback, and decided to do something different. They started selling their mouthwatering chocolates online and ultimately did a booming business. They were able to close the shop, which was losing money, and instead do a tremendous trade online. Yes, the few local customers from the shop were still able to buy their chocolates.

Remember what Helen Keller stated, that when one door closes, another one opens. Life is an adventure, and may include some very rocky roads.

**Seeking Employment**

If you lose your job, as I did in my divorce, or if you have been a stay-at-home mom, here are some tips. Is there a business that you frequent regularly? Maybe it's a coffee shop or small retail store. The employers already know and like you and may want you on their work team. It requires a little nerve, but ask if they would consider you for the next job opening. This is what I did and I got hired on the spot. Or they may be able to steer you in another direction, if they are not presently hiring. Once in a awhile, the fact that you are so nice and seem almost like part of their family can be a drawback. My older son is very close to a couple who own a local restaurant, where he dines regularly. The couple said that they did not want anything to come in the way of their friendship, so they would not hire him. This may happen to you as well.

This could be the time to volunteer. If you have empty hours and you offer to volunteer with a charity organization, they will be able to see firsthand what a good worker you are. If a paid position comes up, you are right there to apply for it. Also, some well-connected volunteers may have other job leads.

Remember other places you patronize, such as the library. Do they have a part-time job available? There are some mothers at a local elementary school who get paid for filling in for the secretary, or doing lunch or playground duty. No, it is not big bucks, but it is something. If you are facing foreclosure or huge divorce fees, jobs you didn't want before will start to look good. Just moving forward with your life will make you feel better and will open up other opportunities.

Some people try temp work, which can lead to a permanent position. This could be the time to do an internship to learn new job skills, thus increasing your marketability. If you do an internship in your field, the staff can give you job leads, if they are not hiring presently. You may want to do an internship or apprenticeship in a totally new area, such as with a florist, to see if a change in careers would be the ticket.

Look in the classified ad section of your newspaper. Perhaps you did not think of a type of job in your area of interest or hobby. Are you great at crafts? Check for a job opening at a bead or knitting shop, if that is your talent. Find a clothing store, if you have a flair for fashion, even if you have never pursued that area before. Think positively, and be creative and flexible. You will find something.

Most likely you will need to spruce up your résumé (CV). Volunteering can be valuable on a résumé, especially if you utilized skills from your degree or work history. My community college has a free résumé service and did an excellent job with mine, including printing it on parchment paper. The adviser there had some job ideas and helped me write two great cover letters. Some teachers provide this service for a reasonable price.

Watch the hilarious movie, "Nine to Five" about madcap antics in the workplace. Dolly Parton and Lily Tomlin are joined by Jane Fonda's recently divorced character, who is at a new job, after a long work hiatus.

# 21

## Secrets of Low Stress Women

Australia *Women's Weekly* magazine (December, 2009) had great information on ways to reduce stress, road tested by Australians. Girlfriends have added additional tips to the list. Quotes are from this magazine.

Be honest; lying adds to stress. "We hide part of ourselves, when we lie about how we feel. The normal stress associated with lying is compounded by the stress of suppressing emotions."

Set aside ten to twenty minutes a day that you will worry. Banish thoughts of worry to this daily time period. Write down your thoughts before you go to sleep and note any actions that you will do the following day.

Be in nature, take a hike, eat your lunch in the park. Studies have indicated "that natural, green settings have the power to reduce anger and aggression and along the way, reduce stress." Blood pressure and stress hormones decrease in this bucolic setting.

When you need help, ask for it. Trying to do everything around the house, your children's school, or work can be an unrealistic goal and can also be a detriment to your health.

Do yoga to clear the mind and strengthen the body. Meditation enables you to be more serene in stressful divorce situations and to analyze information in a calmer manner. Eat dark chocolate (containing antioxidants) and food with magnesium. Pamper yourself with massages, facials and pedicures.

Be immersed in the moment and quiet the inner chatter. When entering Disneyland, there is a sign saying that you are leaving today and entering yesterday, tomorrow and fantasy. What a great reminder to be in the moment, have fun, plus leave your stress and worries of today behind. Enjoy seeing the twinkling lights of London below on the Peter Pan ride. If you are having difficulty being in the moment, concentrate on whatever is happening, as though you will be quizzed on it. Be like your children or younger self and be fully immersed in the situation.

One woman said that if she were in the grocery store, she would be fully present, looking at what she was buying. If doing dishes, then she would be concentrating on that. During your divorce, feel your different senses to be fully present in the situation. Feel the sun on your face, smell the flowers, hear the traffic noises and see the children playing. Relaxation CDs and meditation can help you let go of the mental divorce chatter.

If you have the means and opportunity, get away to a special place to help you relax and be fully present in the moment. Go to a spa with girlfriends. Have your heart rate increased by a roller coaster ride, rather than by the anxiety of worrying about what is just around the corner with your divorce. If you enjoy communing with nature, then make sure to stroll around a park or have a picnic in a leafy area.

## Dealing with Insomnia

You particularly require regular sleep during your divorce, so here are a few tips on beating insomnia, which can result from a myriad of causes.

Talk to a therapist or get out more with friends to share confidences and laughter. Try Yoga, meditation or Tai Chi. Every morning, I do Qi Gong stretches and breathing, which activate energy points. Since practicing it, my back issue is a thing of the past. In 1989, China recognized Qi Gong as a standard of medical treatment and it is currently offered on their National Health Plan. It greatly reduces stress.

Sleep apnea is when breathing stops for a few moments and your brain wakes you up to start breathing again. The muscles in the back of the throat relax and occlude the airway. Sleeping on one's side or in more severe cases, wearing a CPAP mask, can alleviate this condition. Other medical reasons for insomnia include chronic pain or having to get up at night to go to the toilet. Work with your doctor on these issues and limit your liquid intake before bedtime.

Insomnia can be started by worrying, which becomes a habit and a vicious cycle. Break this cycle by having a regular bedtime, with planned winding down and relaxing beforehand. Ditch watching the news before bedtime. The news will still be there in morning. Sleep in a dark, quiet and cool temperature bedroom, with your clock out of your view. When I have a difficult time getting to sleep or if I wake up in the middle of the night, Bach's Sleep Rescue Remedy helps me. Some people write down their worries or the next day's to do list, which allows them to stop worrying and then have uninterrupted sleep.

Psychological issues, such as depression or bipolar disorder, can cause insomnia, as can the medications that treat them. Contact your doctor to adjust your dose or switch to a similar, but different medication. Regular exercise, such as walking, boosts your mood and your endorphins.

## Relaxation, Meditation and Visualization

Buy a relaxation CD, which guides you on how to relax, so you do not have to think about it. I like the ones which start at the feet and move up the body to the head. These CDs have you tense a body part and then totally relax it. You may even fall asleep during this. Other CDs have soothing sounds, like whales or rain. Take some deep breaths to release tension and focus on the sounds.

Meditation can be done in different ways and you may opt to try various methods. A Buddhist monk, Olanda Ananda, who holds seminars globally, has these suggestions. He emphasized concentrating on your breath. Next, realize that you will have thoughts. He said to deal with these thoughts as if they were passing clouds, and just let them drift by. Clear your mind, concentrate on the individual breaths and do not let any thoughts linger. The more you meditate, the easier it becomes to keep your mind serene.

Other forms of meditation include repeating a mantra (a saying or word) or chanting. If you are in an ashram in India, you may be chanting in their language. The purpose of meditation is to still your mind, which helps you to deal with life's situations more calmly. Your blood pressure and heart rate can even decrease with regular practice of these techniques.

Visualization has you relax mentally and go to an inviting place, such as the beach or an Alpine meadow. Sit in a comfortable chair and close your eyes. Take several deep breaths. Inhale tranquility and exhale tension. See tranquility as a color, such as a blue. Exhale tension as a color, such as a dark grey or black. Relax your body, continuing to take deep cleansing breathes, inhaling tranquility blue and exhaling tension dark grey.

For example, mentally walk along the beach and feel the warm, grainy sand under your feet and between your toes. Take a deep breath and inhale the salty air. Feel a gentle breeze ruffle your hair and the warm sunshine on your upturned face. Notice the incredible spectrum of blues and greens of the water. See the foamy waves hitting the shoreline. Hear the roar of the waves and the cries of the sea gulls. Feel moved by the beauty of the scene and the serenity it brings you. You are relaxed. Taste the occasional spray of salt water as it hits your tongue. Involve all of your senses in visualization.

You can go back to this place mentally whenever you want a refuge of calmness and relaxation. Later, when you are entering a courtroom or an attorney's office, go back to your special place. Be there and feel the calmness, bringing this feeling with you into different situations.

Imagine yourself out of pain. Here is a tip from the Neuro-Linguistic Programming (NLP) world to get rid of pain. Think of pain as a color. Maybe your intense headache is a black color. Now give it a shape. For example, you might imagine your headache as black smoke. Next, pick an area of your body that is comfortable and give that feeling a color. Then imagine it as a shape. For instance, the comfortable feeling may be a blue sphere.

Imagine the black smoke of headache pain leaving the top of your head, like black smoke billowing out of a chimney. In its place, move the comfortable blue sphere up through your body, filling up your head with a pleasant sensation. Take some deep breathes, breathing out whatever does not feel good (black smokey headache pain) and breathing in tranquility. Think of a favorite vacation place and do the above visualization exercise. This visualization also works well with kids and helps distract them if they are at the dentist or in other unpleasant situations.

**Language Affecting Body Pain and Injuries**

Notice the words you use and their connection to what body part hurts. Do you say, "She is such a pain in the neck" and wonder why you have chronic neck discomfort? Do not connect your angry words with a specific body location. My teenage son would say, "He really pisses me off," and then developed a problem "pissing" in a public bathroom (medically known as "shy bladder"). After I pointed out the connection between his use of words and his "pissing" problem, the shy bladder became a thing of the past.

I worked in a busy trauma unit and kept saying that I needed a break. Well, I got a nice, long six week break with a broken foot. My subconscious heard that I wanted a break and literally followed that directive. Your subconscious mind is looking for your word choice to give it direction. Just admit to anger or frustration and leave it at that. You have heard, "Be careful what you wish for, because you may get it." Well I sure did.

One older, very healthy family friend kept saying he/she's a "corker" when someone was a bit maddening or out of control. So instead of declaring negatively, "He'll give me a stroke some day," say positively, "He's a corker."

Another aspect of language is to have it point you towards a goal, not what you do not want to do. If your goal is to remember your lunch bag, then say, "I must remember my lunch bag," Not "I cannot forget my lunch bag." You do not want the two words "forget" and "lunch bag" together in your subconscious mind. An example of this concept is when Lindsey's husband was going to Beijing for a business trip and she wanted him to bring her back a t-shirt. Instead of saying what designs she wanted (her goal), she told him what she did not like. Lindsey said, "Bring me back a t-shirt with any scene on it except the Great Wall of China." When Drew got to Beijing, he remembered that Lindsey wanted a t-shirt and had said something about The Great Wall of China. Yes, you guessed right, that is the t-shirt Lindsey received.

**Empowered by Songs**

Decrease stress and fire up your immune system with music. Select songs that soothe you to get you through your stressful divorce. Or, choose tunes to represent your moods and what you are going through. For example, during my difficult divorce, when I heard Tom Petty's, "I won't back down...I'll stand my ground," it motivated me to hang in there and spend the extra time digging through records to prove my points. I felt like I could handle what was thrown at me and "stand my ground." Also, the Tom Petty song, "Don't Come Around Here No More," fits the bill about not wanting to see my ex. My boys said to add, "I Will Survive" (Gloria Gaynor), to my list and yes, I was surviving and that became my mantra. Post-divorce, The Who's "I'm Free" is such an empowering song. Any Aretha Franklin ditty will do, especially "Respect." Pick some songs that represent you and your situation. A great song for any situation, which can turn your stressful day around is "What a Wonderful World" by Louis Armstrong. It is enchanting, with an upbeat message delivered in a musical way.

## Laughter

Laughter reduces stress and raises one's immunity. A higher immunity helps to fight off viruses more efficiently. The New England Journal of Medicine states that laughter reduces the bad cholesterol (LDH) and raises the good cholesterol (HDL). It also reduces blood pressure, and the stress hormone cortisol. Laughter increases the release of endorphins, which are neurotransmitters that help us feel good, like opiates that reduce pain. One acquaintance had TMJ pain and when she had a fit of laughter, the pain completely went away. So go out and enjoy that comedy, because you are boosting your health.

Oxford University did a study where participants either watched a comedy or a documentary. After these shows, the researchers applied either very cold or painful pressure to the subjects' arms. The people who watched the comedies and laughed hard, withstood 10% more pain or cold than the other subjects who did not experience the belly laughs.

When I was in the throes of divorce, I borrowed the movie "First Wives Club" and laughed all the way through it. This film should be a requirement for women going through divorce. I was almost fifty and the actresses, Bette Midler, Diane Keaton and Goldie Hawn, all turned fifty while filming this movie. Besides being hilarious, the message was not revenge, but justice. My two sons heard my laughter, and when I was finished, asked if they could view it also. I put this movie right back in and chuckled through it again, along with my sons.

A great book, also humorous, and with the same message, is Elizabeth Buchan's, *Revenge of the Middle Age Woman*. I had read it previously, but enjoyed it immensely the second time around during my divorce. The character lives in London and loses her husband and job, as I did. This novel is a must read.

## Health Concerns

Stress causes health concerns, and the question arises as to the difference between a panic attack and a heart attack. The classic sign of a heart attack in women is back pain. So many females have said, "I did not have chest or jaw pain, and no pain radiated down my left arm." If you suddenly start having back pain, often accompanied with nausea, get to a hospital. One retired nurse, who later died from a massive MI, waited six hours before calling her daughter while suffering from intense lower back pain and vomiting. The cardiologist said that if she had gotten to the hospital at the onset of these symptoms, her prognosis would have been fairly good.

If a young woman has a history of panic attacks, then that is probably what is happening. A panic attack comes on suddenly, with a feeling of anxiety, breathlessness and mild chest discomfort. Some women have described these being accompanied by a feeling of doom. It is better to go to the hospital with a panic attack, then to err and not go to the ER when it is really a heart attack.

If you suddenly cannot think of common words and have numbness or drooping on one side, this could be the onset of a stroke. Think "star" and have the person do the following to determine the possibility of a stroke:

S smile, to see if it is lopsided.
T tongue, stick out the tongue, to see if it goes to one side.
A arms, hold arms straight out in front, to see if one drops.
R repeat simple phrases.

Get to the ER immediately if any of these are abnormal.

# 22

## Grief

Grief seems to hit a few months to a year after the divorce is finalized and can take women by surprise. Leona said that she wished someone would have told her that after her divorce she would experience grief. Even though Leona left her abusive husband, she still passed through all the stages of grief.

Recognize that you will have grief in some degree, no matter how you feel about your ex. Grief is a sense of loss, whether it is for a person, or a former way of life. Dr. Elisabeth Kubler-Ross explains the grief process in her excellent book, *On Death and Dying*. The stages are "anger, denial, bargaining, depression" (some therapists say the latter is anger turned inwards) and "acceptance." The emotions run into each other and one can shift back and forth between the stages. These stages are pertinent to divorce, or having a major upheaval.

Some friendships may change after your divorce. If there were some abuse in your marriage and you shared that with friends, it is dismaying to discover they still want to maintain relationships with both of you. This is particularly difficult when they were originally your friends and met your ex through you. Divorce tends to separate your true friends from others. You may find that divorce similarly prunes your family tree. Naomi's Aunt Mae does not have children and lives across the country from her. During visits, Naomi would spend a lot of time with Aunt Mae, who definitely prefers male to female company. After the divorce, this aunt came to town and stayed in a hotel, choosing to spend time with Naomi's ex and his family. She said that they entertained her so much that she was too tired to get together with Naomi and her children. A loss or change in relationships post-divorce is one more part of this grief. Understand that this will happen in varying degrees.

Grief does lessen with time, whether it is with divorce or death. Emma wished that someone would have told her that there is a "light at the end of the tunnel," and that the pain of divorce diminishes. Kelly echoed this wish with, "I would have liked to have known that the pain would eventually go away."

A person can get stuck in one stage, benefiting from a therapist, a life coach or a support group. This section gives ways of dealing with grief.

Exercise, eat nutritious food and get plenty of rest.

Help yourself emotionally by getting outside to a park or going hiking.

Get a massage, facial or pedicure.

Vent your anger/sadness.

Realize that holidays can have unrealistic expectations—entertaining, spending increased time with family, putting on a cheerful holiday face when that is not how you really feel. You may be grieving for your old way of life, and this may be more painful during the holiday season. Express your needs and feelings to others and ask for their support.

Dopamine, a neurotransmitter which helps regulate emotion, is increased when one falls in love, does something enjoyable or has a new adventure. So, if your ex is still living in your head rent-free, do something new to increase your dopamine level. Take a fun class, such as Zumba, up your exercise time or go to an exotic destination. Looking at your ex's photos, checking his Facebook page or reading old love letters will not help you to move on. Get rid of, or at least gather up photos and mementos and store them out-of-sight. Even better would be to get rid of them or take them to your parents' house to deal with at a later time. Naomi had a few nice family photos with her ex in them. She skillfully edited her ex right out of them and can enjoy these pictures now.

One British woman wrote about her charmed life in a beautiful country village. She loved volunteering, being in the community and spending time with her neighbors. When her husband suddenly left her, she went through the stages of grief until she eventually reached the stage of acceptance and hope. This Brit learned to accept and deal with the reality of her situation. She moved to London, got a job, met new neighbors and started looking forward to planning things for the future. She found joy in life and put the painful past behind her.

# 23

## Happiness and Positive Change

*"The greater part of our happiness or misery depends*
*upon our dispositions and not by our circumstances."*
—*Martha Washington*

The December, 2009 issue of Australia's *Women's Weekly* magazine presented research results on the topic of happiness. This magazine stated that studies on identical twins raised in different homes found that they "have similar levels of life satisfaction." The results suggested that there existed a genetic component to happiness. Some researchers stipulate that there is a "set point" of happiness. We dip below this set point during troubling times, such as going through a divorce, but bounce back to this point at a later time. This explains why some people seem to see the world through rose colored glasses, while others view it as the glass half empty.

Australian Professor Robert Cummins does not view this as a negative, but instead feels that we all operate on a particular level of happiness. He says that people "can build resilience to the knocks in life by marrying a supportive partner or having enough savings to weather a storm" when they have a lower set point of happiness.

Happiness can affect recovery in catastrophic circumstances. An example is given of a young woman who was in a major auto accident, wheelchair-bound for life. She took stock of her situation, regarding what she could and could not do, and got on with life, striving for what was possible. This gal surprised people with such a positive outlook. She got married, had children and currently has a fulfilling career. Look at how positive Christopher Reeves was and how he became the inspiration for quads and paraplegics through the energy he put into his endeavors to improve his quality of life.

You can choose to be a positive person and enjoy life, or to be miserable. On a TV episode of "Forensic Files," a woman's husband hired hit men to kill her. She sustained almost fatal injuries, pulling through it, although paralyzed from the neck down. You might think she would have felt like a victim or a prisoner in her wheelchair, but that was not the case. Instead she stated what fun things she was doing now and how she was having the time to really enjoy life. Once a week she goes out to listen to jazz with her girlfriends, and she has a long list of other great activities that she does. It is your choice how you decide to approach life.

Nelson Mandela could have felt bitter and trapped during his long prison term. No, people could not imprison his mind or spirit. You control your happiness and the meaning you find in life. A Buddhist proverb states "Pain is inevitable, but suffering is optional."

Australian Dr. Timothy Sharp says that happiness is in people's control, and research shows that we "can bump up our long-term happiness by having enriching relationships, developing goals and contemplating what we want out of life."

Buddhist philosophy says that when you are faced with adverse circumstances, feeling unhappy serves no purpose in overcoming the undesirable situation. Instead, it increases your anxiety. Anxiety and unhappiness affect your sleep patterns, your appetite and your health. If nothing can be done to resolve the difficulty (as in divorce situations), it is useless to feel unhappy about it.

Roads to happiness include having goals in life, delving into spirituality and doing community service. Having friends and social interactions increase one's happiness and the feeling of having meaning in one's life. There are ways to amp up your happiness, such as doing good deeds every day and being thankful for what you have.

When you have just come from a court hearing or unpleasant dealings with your soon to be ex, try these suggestions. Let a car, which is trying to enter a line of traffic, get in front of you. Return a shopping cart for an elderly person, after she has unloaded her groceries. Let a woman with a crying baby get ahead of you in the grocery line. Notice how you can help someone in a small way. Their thanks and smiles really give your mood a positive boost.

## Gratitude

Various people have commented on how powerful the act of gratitude is to one's well being. Everyday write down a certain number (3 to 10) of things you are thankful for that happened that day. It could be the kindness of strangers, seeing butterflies, or finding money in the street. It does not matter how big or small these are. What this process does is to change your focus to the positives in your daily life. Your attention is drawn to what is pleasant, instead of dwelling on the negatives. After doing this for at least a week, I noticed that the flowers around my neighborhood seemed brighter. I observed different birds and more butterflies. People appeared to be smiling at me more, or maybe I did not notice that as much earlier.

Some women opt to take photos of what they are thankful for in their lives and keep them as reminders. This could be a luscious latte, as one woman did who was grateful for her local coffee shop. Many snapshots are of family members and beautiful scenes of nature. An activity in Australia which is gaining in popularity is to take pictures on a daily basis to remind people to pause and enjoy life.

Reflect on the small pleasures around you. I was walking around our neighborhood with a friend and we stopped to enjoy an impromptu concert. A bird, sitting in the treetop, was singing her heart out with a beautiful melody. Any disappointments of that day were quickly forgotten and replaced with this lovely experience.

## Be Happy, Live Longer and Better

There was a study done a few years back to see if feeling and acting younger impacted one's health. Men were divided into two groups and spent different weeks at a lodge. The control group watched current movies, TV shows and news, then discussed what was happening in their lives.

The other group of men had strict instructions to act as though they were living in a certain year, which was about 30 years in the past. The TV shows, movies and news broadcasts were just what would have been seen in that particular year. These men were only allowed to talk about their personal lives and world events from that year, or earlier. If they were dating then, that girl was discussed, but not their future marriage. These fellows talked about sports and other interests from that era.

Extensive blood work and tests were performed before and after the week at the lodge with both groups. The guys in the control group may have been a little more relaxed afterward, but significant medical changes were not found.

However, there was a measurable difference in the immune system, cardiac function, blood pressure and other body systems in the men who lived a week in the past. There was a marked decrease in arthritic pain and other complaints, with a surge in energy. The researchers said they were amazed by how much the health of the men had improved in the second group.

Get in touch with your younger self and remember your passions and interests. Watch those old reruns of your favorite TV shows, like "I Love Lucy." Talk about the good old times with your pals. Notice your increase in energy and how those aches and pains diminish. One article that I read recently stated that those people who feel younger actually can increase their lifespan by ten years.

# 24

## Moving On

### Forgiveness

This chapter is about getting unstuck and moving on to a more fulfilling life during and post-divorce. Forgiveness is about setting yourself free, not about the other person. You forgive and do not have to let the other person know that you did so, or even see him again. It is about cutting free any ties that bind you to certain situations or people and letting go of the past. You have read in the papers how parents have forgiven their child's murderer, and you probably wondered if they were saints or nuts. What these parents did was to let go of bitterness, anger and any other attachments, so that they could get over this tragedy and move on with their lives.

*Webster's Dictionary* defines "forgiveness" as "To cease to feel resentment against one's enemies." Not forgiving is a way to stay attached to your ex and remain stuck in resentment and bitterness. Not forgiving is maintaining a tie to him and leaves you shut off to future relationships. Forgiveness severs the hurt/injustice which binds you both together. Forgiveness is just about letting go and not about getting revenge. Thoughts of revenge keep you connected to that person.

Author Catherine Ponder in her book, *Open Your Mind to Prosperity*, recommends saying this affirmation to help let go of toxic people or situations: "I now release and am released from everything and everybody that are no longer part of the Divine Plan for my life. Everything and everybody that are no longer part of the Divine Plan for my life now release me." What is nice about this affirmation is that it is a two way street, because you are stating for your ex to cut ties with you as well. I wrote this on a colored index card with a vibrant felt pen and propped it up by my bathroom mirror, so I could say this several times a day. I still revisit this affirmation when angry thoughts about my ex pop up out of nowhere.

Affirmations are positive statements that you can make about what you want out of life in a myriad of situations. What you are doing is working with your subconscious mind and a Higher Power (whatever is in your belief system) to move you towards change. Any Catherine Ponder book is chock full of affirmations that I tweak to fit my individual situation. You can make specific ones, such as about your next court date having a positive outcome or that you get "xyz" with the property division. Some affirmations that worked for me are:

"Divine guidance is now showing me the way to...(insert your situation, such as an amicable divorce). Divine Guidance is working through me and all concerned to bring about the perfect outcome now."

"All financial doors are open to me now and are manifesting abundance in expected and unexpected ways. God is bringing me wealth and opportunities and I give thanks for them."

It is important to forgive yourself, so that you can heal and move on, and not remain mired in the past. You did the best that you could with the life skills and knowledge that you possessed at that time. Louise L. Hay has a great book, *The Power is Within You*, which teaches you how to forgive yourself and others and not repeat destructive patterns of your past. She recommends saying to yourself, "I'm doing the best that I can and even though I'm in a pickle now, I will get out of it somehow, so let's find the best way to do it."

Forgiveness is the first step to change. Understanding and love come after this, so that destructive patterns of the past can be altered or eliminated.

## Justice, Not Revenge

A great life guide is the Law of Karma, which is the law of cause and effect, not punishment. It parallels biblical verses, such as "What you sow, so shall you reap." Another is, "What goes around comes around," and also The Golden Rule. If your gossip and actions cause misery for others, do not be surprised when misery comes knocking on your door. Allow Karma to do its thing, not you.

When someone has dealt you a cruel blow, do not plot revenge. You have heard of road rage, where people want to dish out revenge on the spot, sometimes with fatal results. It is karma that will come back to you and not add to your happiness. Think of the cliché, "It's like water rolling off a duck's back," and let those insults roll off you. It is not worth having a stroke or a heart attack to prove that you are right. Your body responds to thoughts and images as if they were real. Save your health and realize that they are the ones with problems. Use this affirmation: "Divine Justice is doing Its work in this situation now."

You attract what you are, not what you want. If you want to be around positive, kind people, then be that yourself. If we do not change, then our problems go with us. When people move across the country to get away from problems, in reality they are packing these woes with them. Life will keep repeating the same experiences or types of relationships until we master that lesson and move on. Here are some questions to ask yourself: Do you accept personal responsibility or is it always someone else's fault? Are you focused on spiritual growth or selfish gain? Are you ruled by monetary goals and instant gratification? Do you learn from your personal history?

Helion Publishing produces wonderful credit card-size cards of information on many different subjects, such as karma and even reflexology that can act as daily reminders to support positive behavior.

## Like Attracts Like

If you want to know what someone is really like, look at his friends. There is truth to "Birds of a feather stick together." An obvious example is that of gang members, and what they have in common is not pretty. Post-divorce, if you meet a guy, but he has friends who are disrespectful of women or animals, think again. This bloke may be covering up what he is really like in order to get closer to you.

Naomi was dating this very nice PhD-bound student from a loving family. She could just imagine them as in-laws and kept making excuses for some odd behaviors from her boyfriend. When Naomi pointed out discrepancies (lies), he always had a reason, and usually it was someone else's fault. Then Naomi took a hard look at her boyfriend's buddies. Some were out picking up girls while in committed relationships. She met his mentor professor, who was so into hardcore porn (before the Internet), that it slowly dawned on her what was transpiring, as her guy became more belittling and worse. It was difficult, but she broke up with him and learned to check out the people around potential boyfriends. Are they ethical or jerks? Is there an acquaintance that puts you off a bit? Maybe there is a darkness inside of him that attracts the same type of friends. Abigail Van Buren (Dear Abby) stated, "The best index to a person's character is how he treats people who can't do him any good and how he treats people who can't fight back." This is an important concept for post-divorce dating.

Another post-divorce dating concern is this. Do you follow a pattern of being with the same type of guy? Is your soon-to-be-ex similar to former boyfriends? Deidre's father was a sociopath and she married one as well. Deidre's former fiance also had his issues and problems. Sociopaths can be quite charming, yet are manipulative. Her friends gently suggested that if she decided to date again, to be very careful and possibly see a counselor.

A woman I met during my divorce recommends that divorcees wed widowers who have been happily married. As a veteran of a contemptuous divorce, she remarried one of these men and said that they "don't carry all of the baggage and bitterness" that many divorced men do the second time around. An added bonus is that she is not drawn into a battle with any exes. Juliette, a charming southern belle in her 60s, echoed this same sentiment. Juliette is blissfully wedded to a widower, who had been happily married the first time around.

## With Toxic People, Just Say "Good-bye"

You are more vulnerable during and when recently divorced, which may affect your judgment. Feel free to avoid or limit contact with people with whom you are uncomfortable. Forensic Files on TV is full of true stories about people who were too polite to say, "Good-bye." If you feel awkward around someone, then do not let them into your house, as one sister-in-law did. Her brother-in-law killed the woman, with her two young children present. She had told many people, including her parents, that she felt unsafe around this man. Another case was about a high school honor student who accepted a ride with a neighbor and never arrived home. Do not waste time or energy talking to these toxic people. It is not worth your safety to be polite.

Recently, on "Forensic Files," a high school girl rejected a creepy classmate, Jack, and ended up marrying a nice guy. Jack never married and continued to have contact with this couple and later on, their two children. Her daughter realized what a creep Jack was and kept her distance. The son looked up to Jack as an unofficial godfather, even taking trips with him, as an older teenager. Well, Jack had the son put him down as a beneficiary to the kid's life insurance policy, then rigged the murder to look like an accident. Luckily,

Jack was eventually caught and got a life sentence. My point is why did the high school girl—then later a mother—allow this nut case to be around her family? A restraining order would have been helpful to protect her children. Sometimes we are trying to be kind to someone we should not even feel sorry for, or much worse, allow contact with our children.

Unfortunately, I fell into this same trap, to a much lesser degree. I had a professional relationship with a couple, who did not have any children and I felt especially sorry for the female. She and I had lunch, even though I did not really like her. Then she and her husband started buying small gifts for my sons and wanted to present them in person, at kid-friendly cafes. My kids were polite, but did not want contact with this couple. I was in a bad marriage, so was very vulnerable and not making the best decisions. When I finally figured out what this couple was really like, I broke off all contact, and my children were relieved. If your intuition tells you something is not right with very needy or friendly people, keep them away from your kids. I was too trusting of people during my divorce and recently afterward, so keep this issue in mind.

If you are hanging onto too many people, whom you only see out of habit, you may not have room for more meaningful relationships to enter your life. Limit your time with energy vampires who drain you, and spend it with positive people instead.

**Your Parents**

Accept your parents and move on with your life. Many of us seek in new relationships what we did not receive from our parents. In *British Psychologies* magazine, Nicole Prieur writes about this issue. She states that when we are small children, we base our preconceptions on the world from what we received and did not receive from our parents (such as attention, love, and having basic needs met). "What did my existence mean to my parents?" affects all areas of our adult life, particularly at family gatherings.

As part of getting unstuck, we go through the "anger stage." We realize that our family is not perfect and they that will never be able to meet all of our needs. Nicole Prieur states that the next stage is "adolescence," when we push hard to get our needs met. Some people never move on from this stage, going through life demanding that friends and partners give them what their parents could not. I have met plenty of elderly boys still stuck in this stage. The third stage is when we learn to "accept that what we did not get as children, we are never going to get from our parents," so we should stop being angry with them. Nicole Prieur writes that we take on "family pressure" to be the good girl, or to be able to take over the family business. Part of becoming adults is to realize that we cannot satisfy our parents' ambitions and must do what is best for us. We have to overcome any feelings of guilt in not becoming what our parents had in mind. By becoming free, truly being what we want to be, then we can appreciate what we did get and learn from our parents.

You can change your reactions and behavior, not someone else's. Refuse to participate in old childhood patterns. If the same arguments erupt, remove yourself by taking a walk, or change your response. Try being nonchalant like, "Yeah, perhaps I do," and change the subject. Act bored or laid back, so the family sees that they cannot get a rise out of you. Make a joke or bring humor to the situation. If things are truly awful, then leave.

# 25

## Post-Divorce Advice

Notify acquaintances of your new post-divorce status when you bump into them, if you prefer not to make a general announcement. I would immediately tell people I had not seen in awhile that I was happily divorced, revealing how my sons' lives were wonderful. If a strange look were given, I would proceed to relay that my sons gave me flowers and chocolates on my divorce anniversary. A few women babbled, "I am so sorry," and I would ask them whatever for, since I just said how much better my sons and I are doing post-divorce.

If you are grieving or upset, a simple, "We got divorced. How are you?" will suffice. You do not owe anyone an explanation or graphic details regarding your divorce situation. Smile and remark, "I have moved on," whether or not you really have.

### Financial

Post-divorce, develop a budget, even if it is the first time that you have ever done so. Keep an expense diary to see where every penny goes for at least two weeks. Look at your alimony and salary to set up a reasonable budget with a savings plan. By examining your financial diary, it will make it easier to see where to cut out some expenses. This may be the time to do a consultation with a financial adviser that charges a set fee for service, rather than a commission. Some less ethical advisers pick investments that give themselves more money, rather than what is best for you, the client. I had a stock broker working mainly on commission, who picked out a lousy annuity, because she got more money for it. The financial adviser can look at your expense diary and help you pinpoint where your money is going, plus devise savvy money-saving strategies. An Arabian proverb states that if you only have two coins, spend one on food and the other one on flowers. One nourishes your body and the other one, your soul.

## New Divorce Trends

I had the idea of the "divorce ring." I had a loose gemstone mounted in a ring that I designed and designated as my divorce one. The shop owners liked the concept tremendously and started to promote this trend. Yes, some divorces are sad events, leaving broken hearts, but others are "I'm so glad I escaped" ones.

A new trend is celebrating your divorce with a party. One photo in the news pictured a tiered cake with a bride on top and a groom at the bottom. Where I live, more and more women are having blow out parties to celebrate their divorces. One ex-wife hired a limo to take her girlfriends to a nearby city to party until the wee hours of the morning. After my divorce was finalized, my friends took me out for lattes or lunches over the following two months. My out-of-town-pals sent me cards to commemorate this happy occasion.

You also have had people and support on this journey to divorce. Emma Pritchard stated in the November, 2011, *Woman and Home Magazine*, "People always see divorce as a negative experience, but for me it's liberating. It's given me the confidence to achieve things I'd never imagined." Gina wished she had known she would emerge stronger after going through the turmoil of divorce. This is like metal becoming stronger after going through fire in the process of becoming a sword.

I hope this book enables you to gain insight on many issues that may have plagued you for years. It spells out how destructive ideas and actions can directly affect your health and well-being, providing a blueprint for self change. Specific strategies are given for dealing with many aspects of your divorce, from obtaining cash and slashing costs to dealing with relationships. Relationships are not static, but change with divorce, and you can only alter your own actions, not someone else's behavior. You are stronger than you envision, and if you follow some of the suggestions offered here, you will emerge from this stressful episode of your life as a more powerful person.

# 26

## Recommended Reading and Movies

**Magazines:**

My favorite magazines are *Woman and Home* and the *British Good Housekeeping*. There is a lot less fluff in these British ones and more practical advice than in many other magazines. They have inspiring articles on how women survived adversities and are now thriving. I also have a subscription to *The Australian Women's Weekly Magazine* for the same reasons, plus it is fun to get different viewpoints. Authors Professor Robert Cummins and Dr. Timothy Sharp write for *Australian Women's Weekly Magazine*. Lucy Beresford and Nicole Prieur are in UK's *Pyschologies Magazine*. Emma Pritchard writes for *Woman and Home*. I especially enjoy reading these foreign magazines before holidays to discover their rituals and recipes. It is my splurge.

Additional informative magazines that provide insight and guidance are also listed below:

> *Woman and Home*, British Edition published by IPC Media, Ltd.
> *The Australian Women's Weekly*, published by ACP Magazines, a
>     division of Nine Entertainment Co.
> *Good Housekeeping*, British Edition, published by The National
>     Magazine Company, Ltd. *Psychologies-UK*, Published by Hearst
>     Magazines UK, trading name of the National Magazine Co. Ltd.
> *Red UK Edition*, Hearst Magazines UK is the trading name of the
>     National Magazine Company, Ltd.
> *O, The Oprah Magazine*, published by Harpo Productions
> *Real Simple*, published by Time, Inc., Lifestyle Group
> *Whole Living*, published by Martha Stewart Living Omni Media, Inc.

**Books:**

These books are informative and can point you in the right direction:

Buchan, Elizabeth. *Revenge of the Middle Age Woman*. Penguin, 2003.

Ponder, Catherine. *Open Your Mind to Prosperity*. Marina Del Rey: DeVorss & Co. Publisher, 1971.

Ponder, Catherine. *The Prosperity Secrets of the Ages*. Marina Del Rey: DeVorss & Co. Publisher, 1964.

Ponder, Catherine. *The Healing Secrets of the Ages*. Marina Del Rey: DeVorss & Co. Publisher, 1967.

Ponder, Catherine. *The Dynamic Laws of Healing*. Marina Del Rey: DeVorss & Co. Publisher, 1966.

Hay, Louise L. *The Power is Within You*. Carlsbad, CA: Hay House, Inc.,1991.

Hill, Napoleon. *Think and Grow Rich*. Hollywood, CA: Wilshire Book Co.,1937.

Peale, Norman Vincent. *The Power of Positive Thinking*. New York: Simon & Schuster, 1952.

Grants, Corrine. *Lessons in Letting Go: Confessions of a Hoarder*. Published by Allen & Unmin, 2010.

Any financial book by Suze Orman which is published by Three Rivers Press in New York.

Helion Publishing, Box 52836, Tulsa, OK 74152 They produce wonderful credit card size information on a variety of subjects, such as karma.

**Movies:**

These movies are fun to watch and you can learn a few pointers from them.

"The First Wives Club," 1996.
"Nine to Five," 1980.
"The War of the Roses," 1989.
"Starting Over," 1979.
Watch any comedies, such as: "Tootsie," "If it's Tuesday it Must be Belgium," "It's a Mad Mad Mad Mad World," Laurel and Hardy, "The Wedding Singer" and whatever else tickles your fancy.

CPSIA information can be obtained at www.ICGtesting.com
Printed in the USA
LVOW08s1117260913

354243LV00005B/8/P